I0083112

DONUM

Creating a Sustainable Gifting Experience

By Tracey Alexandria Lynch
WITH Roderic A. Strozier, II

FOREWORD BY KIM CLARK

Edited by Mia DeLaRosa

Enhanced DNA
DEVELOP. NURTURE. ACHIEVE.
Publishing Division

Enhanced DNA Publishing
DenolaBurton@EnhancedDNA1.com
317-537-1438

DONUM: Creating a Sustainable Gifting Experience

Copyright © 2022 Tracey Alexandria Lynch WITH Roderic A. Strozier, II

All rights reserved.

No portion of this publication may be reproduced, stored in any electronic system, or transmitted in any form or by any means without the written permission from the author. Brief quotations may be used in literary reviews.

ISBN-13: 978-1-7378090-9-8

DEDICATION

For my *MITA* (Man in the Arena), my Energy Messenger, the Listener of all ideas, my husband, co-creator, and truest partner, Darrell Lee Vardiman.

To my father, Walter Elijah Lynch, my original MITA.

And to all the problem solvers who dearly love our planet home.

And thank you to our tribe that helped make this project possible: Anne Christ, Denola Burton, Mia DeLaRosa, Michelle Ruben, and Levi Osborn.

♥

T. Lynch & R. Strozier

FOREWORD
By
Kim Clark

I believe everyone wants to be a helper. When I ask someone if they can help me, I almost always get a YES! This book will give you a new perspective. It will recalibrate your beliefs about your role in changing the world by making it cleaner. We can stop the surge of global warming and climate change for our children and grandchildren. The message is vital, timely, and rather unexpected, as the solution is fresh and new. Open your mind to how you can easily be a helper.

Donum is an important book that is urgently needed. Its message is simple, and its solution to our modern-day issues contributing to global warming and climate change is timely. Donum is a much-needed, right-now message. I am not a doomsdayer, but I can identify a crisis with a looming tipping point. And as a teacher, I know this is a message we must share with every generation because they *need* to hear it. While I'm confident that adults will shift their behaviors out of self-preservation, I believe it is our youth that will harness the power necessary to transform the generational expectations surrounding gifting.

Tracey Lynch is an entrepreneur, teacher, broad thinker, and friend of this planet. It is easy to see how her son, Rod, evolved into a profound thinker and human being. They both live as examples of the work between these pages. I am proud to call her my friend. She intently and presently listens and can artfully synthesize information and varied perspectives into ideas that can remedy issues that create a benefit for us all. Tracey can look at big problems and easily pick them apart. By employing simple answers that require the least amount of work, offer the least inconvenience, and allow the path of least resistance to unfold, Tracey devises solutions that are easy to implement. She has an artful way of doing all this without making anyone feel less intelligent, wrong, or inadequate. Maya Angelou once said, "When you know better, you do better." This book's main objective is to do just that.

By shining a light on our planet's current situation, we can more easily illuminate a path of correction. I believe we will be successful in pulling off this magnificent feat. I believe this work will give way to additional inspiring ideas that make subsequent progress possible. This book is easy to read and understand, and its principle idea is easy to implement.

She and I were recently discussing the deteriorating water levels of the Mississippi and Colorado rivers. The Mississippi River has reached treacherously low conditions, making the passage of shipping barges unsafe and sometimes impossible. We count on the Mississippi River for grain, food, vehicles, and other products just as the Colorado River provides jobs for over 16 million people, irrigation for farms, and drinking water for tens of millions living in the West. Tracey wasn't upset. She knows there is an answer and has an unshakeable faith that we will rise to the occasion with our improved actions, intelligence, innovation, and science to ensure the health of the future planet that our children and grandchildren will inherit.

Her faith is contagious, and this book is just one example of what we can expect from her. I hope as you read, you will feel enlightened, inspired, and motivated to act. The user-friendly principles to increase conscious gifting laid out by Tracey are sure to increase global participation in preserving our planet. Within these pages lies an easy answer to a big problem. I hope you will join in and spread the word of *Donum*.

– Kim Clark

Greenfield, Indiana

T. Lynch & R. Strozier

INTRODUCTION

Why We Wrote This Book

Donum: Latin word meaning gift[1], present[2], or offering[3]

"Climate change is the single greatest threat to a sustainable future but, at the same time, addressing the climate challenge presents a golden opportunity to promote prosperity, security and a brighter future for all."

–Ban Ki-Moon, Former Secretary–General of the United Nations

"Everything we own that's made, sold, shipped, stored, cleaned, and ultimately thrown away does some environmental harm every step of the way, harm that we're either directly responsible for or is done on our behalf."

–Yvon Chouinard, Let My People Go Surfing: The Education of a Reluctant Businessman

Donum is Latin for the word, *gift*. Donum products, including this book, the IOS and Android application, and Donum's permanent replacements for disposable single-use items, are designed to be gifts of knowledge as well as tools that will transform the gifting culture as we know it. Each time we acknowledge our unsustainable habits and act differently in that moment, we plant seeds toward our *better doing*.

One Simple Idea

This is a book about one straightforward idea that, if adopted into our collective consciousness, can change our beliefs about gifting. Donum will shift our understanding of what happens when we return merchandise and of the implausible reverse logistic systems that do not work.

The gift-giving experience, as we know it, is not healthy for our planet. The proof is out there: in factories, wrapped in plastic, packed in foam peanuts and egg crates, packed into foam or cardboard boxes, loaded onto pallets, aboard diesel or coal-burning ships crossing the Atlantic and Pacific, stored in temperature-controlled factories for distribution, on trucks, on trains, on airplanes, to be sorted for its final destination by UPS, DHL, USPS, FedEx, and courier services, landing on our porches and in our mailboxes demanded and satisfied on such a grand scale that our desire for endless choices and access grows exponentially.

Resources, whether they be plants, animals, fabric, polymers, plastics, fiberglass, metallics, minerals, paper, glass, crude, or rubber, the components of products begin their journey somewhere inside of or on our planet. We discover resources, tap them, harvest, and funnel them into the industries that require them to create their products. So far, it has worked out well. Over the past few generations, distribution channels have been relatively healthy, meaning we have been able to order and receive goods in a relatively short time at a fair price. We are now, in 2022, beginning to see a breakdown in distribution due to shortages of foreign and domestic labor, fuel costs, increased expenses associated with transporting goods, etc. Now we are experiencing distribution issues due to drought and diminishing waterways. The shipping capacity has decreased on rivers because the channels are no longer deep enough to support heavier cargo demands. Nevertheless, products complete their mostly standardized, organized, timely, and dependable journey toward consumers' doorsteps.

With the endless choices we have, we can now make more of them. The more options we have and the more choices we make, the greater our chance of making the wrong ones. Say you make no decisions today, which is impossible, but if it were, you would have a zero-percent chance of making an incorrect or poor judgment – because you made no decisions. But if you make 100 choices today, the chances of missing the mark obviously increases.

This phenomenon of decision fatigue happens in our

consumer choices and is now occurring at record levels, but the problem isn't necessarily our hunger for options. The problem isn't necessarily consumerism or capitalism. Our incorrect choices of what to buy for ourselves and others cause the problem of getting returned products back where they came from. Most consumers are not consciously contributing to this problem; we are just making lazy, uninformed choices. We are guessing and assuming, which causes a backlog. See, the system for distributing goods and services was designed to move in one direction, and that direction is from the manufacturer *to* the consumer. The distribution channels were never intended to work in reverse – from the consumer *back* to the manufacturer or seller. This profound yet straightforward fact is the premise for this book.

Expecting the distribution channels to absorb the results of our overindulgence in the holiday spirit, misgifting, or trigger-happy online buying fingers is like listening to your favorite radio station and talking back to the DJ and expecting them to hear you. That signal is emitted one way, and that is *to* you – not from you. You get to choose what you are listening to, and you can easily turn the radio dial. As consumers, that is the action we need to take; we need to change the station we are listening to. We need to understand what our decisions are costing our planet. And to do that, we need to shift our human consciousness in the same direction simultaneously. Let's be clear. We are not asking anyone to stop buying gifts. Gifts are awesome. Gifting is a part of many customs and family traditions.

Participating in the gifting process can be a beautiful and pleasing experience, but when done incorrectly, it wreaks havoc.

We are going to take a look at how to properly purchase a gift with the goal of delivering 100% satisfaction to the recipient every time.

This book aims to help you see that havoc so we can illuminate and understand the repercussions of poor, uniformed gift-giving, which we call *misgifting*. With that insight, we can reshape our thoughts and behaviors to create a more intentional way of gifting. We want to responsibly contribute to those we care for, enjoy the traditions we've come to love, and care for the planet that serves and houses us all. We don't want to focus on how our participation in holiday shopping has changed, how much we spend on gifts, or how much we *should* spend. This book focuses on becoming a responsible global citizen by honing our gift-giving skills and developing the art of thoughtful, sustainable gifting.

Hospitals send parents home with babies all the time. There aren't any rules. Parents receive no parenting manual. There is no one right way to feed, clothe, house, or raise a child. There are a million different ways to do it. Likewise, no one ever sat us down and taught us how to approach purchasing a gift. There are millions of buying options along with a million ways to wrap and present gifts. And, most fortunately, there are millions of ways to save our planet from irresponsible gifting. Those millions of ways have now *called* us, and those millions of ways are called *us*.

We are going to take a look at how to properly purchase a gift that delivers 100% satisfaction to the recipient every time. Issues caused by less thoughtful gifting do not just impact us during the Christmas holiday. It is important to remember to create a sustainable gifting experience throughout the year, including birthdays, Mother's Day, Father's Day, Easter, anniversaries, Valentine's Day, and all of the wonderful "just because I was thinking of you" moments you ever encounter.

It was our desire to write a straightforward book centered around one solution. You shouldn't encounter too much fluff, which means there is little need to skim. It only contains idea-shifting information presented with the purpose of rewiring our brains and societies to do this one super impactful thing differently. And if we collectively do it, which we believe we will, we will transform the world as we know it.

Sometimes you find your path, and sometimes your path finds you. Regarding this book and its message, we believe our path found us. It is an extension of who we already are — a culmination of the seeds that were sown and grown in us. We've traced our history back to the early 1400s, and you know what we found? We found farmers, enslaved people, horticulturists, politicians, inventors, community builders, attorneys, laborers, writers, orators, and teachers. What a combination of history that landed us, a mother and son, in this space to share this message with the world! We are so excited about our path and our decisions. We buy responsibly, opting for second-hand items and quality products designed to last. We refuse most one-use products at restaurants and challenge ourselves to make products and supplies last longer. We use high-quality filters instead of buying bottled water. We compost, conserve, and weatherproof. We reuse, repurpose, recycle, and garden. We can fruit, dehydrate veggies, and freeze our food. We keep our vehicle's tires properly inflated and balanced to avoid wasting fuel. We keep our home's thermostat on a timer, replace our furnace filter like clockwork, lower our water heater temperature to save gas, and we registered ourselves on the no junk mail list. One day, we plan to live off the grid on a beautiful, green, and fully sustainable community property. That's what *we* do, and we know that is a lot to ask. While all these great efforts will contribute to our planet's health, we only ask you to begin with *one step*: shift your mindset about gifting.

Proceeds from the sale of this book support the Donum gifting app and the development of more sustainable everyday products designed to create more thoughtful shoppers and sustainable gifting experiences for you and your tribe. The proceeds from the sale of those sustainable products go back into the community to fund children's programs, autism education, and other community nonprofits. Our goal is to collectively solve *local* problems by first facing our *global* issues. We can extend the life of the planet as we better educate and equip the children for whom we are saving it. We are so excited about this and hope you are too! We believe this book magnifies an existing concept and organizes us all to do one simple thing. You have the power in your hands right now to heal *the planet*. Let's do this!

— Tracey Lynch and Rod Strozier

CONTENTS

*The **first step** to creating a sustainable gifting experience is understanding the importance of sustainable gifting and why it matters. This means understanding the problems we face.*

*The **second step** in creating a sustainable gifting experience is understanding why we do what we do so that we can change our behavior. Until we internalize the why, we will not see value, and if we do not see value, we will not evolve.*

*The **third step** in creating a sustainable gifting experience is identifying actions and tools that will allow us to change most effectively. In today's culture, that means easily, quickly, and non-invasively.*

CHAPTER FOUR – How to Buy a Gift

*The **fourth step** in creating a sustainable gifting experience is to learn how to shop for the recipient. This involves removing your opinions, values, and preferences about what other people want and what's best for their lifestyles. We modernize our behavior by responsibly decreasing the parts of our traditional gifting habits that no longer serve us.*

CHAPTER FIVE – Sustainable Everyday Gifting Ideas

*The **fifth step** in creating a sustainable gifting experience is to be crystal clear about what your tribe wants, while also communicating your specific desires. Otherwise, you are all shooting in the dark and contributing to landfills full of unwanted gifts.*

CHAPTER SIX – Message from My Father

*The **sixth step** in creating a sustainable gifting experience is accepting a new seat in our collective consciousness where things have simply changed, and we must also.*

CHAPTER SEVEN – The Final Say, Message from Mother Earth

*The **seventh step** to creating a sustainable gifting experience is acknowledging what the planet is saying to us right now. We must listen, digest, and process her needs, then take action. By doing this, we* *remain connected to the purpose of sustainability and why it matters. This connection will reinforce our modern gifting behaviors.*

ACKNOWLEDGMENTS

Our Environmental Heroes

INDEX

Sustainable Charitable Giving Opportunities

Companies Offering Sustainable Products: Sustainable Gift Ideas

ENDNOTES

T. Lynch & R. Strozier

CHAPTER ONE

The Issue

"The world is reaching the tipping point beyond which climate change may become irreversible. If this happens, we risk denying present and future generations the right to a healthy and sustainable planet – the whole of humanity stands to lose."

– Kofi Annan, Former Secretary-General of the United Nations

Climate change affects the social and environmental determinants of health – clean air, safe drinking water, sufficient food, and secure shelter. The direct damage costs to health (i.e., excluding costs in health-determining sectors such as agriculture, water, and sanitation) are estimated to be between USD 2 - 4 billion per year by 2030.

– The World Health Organization (October 2021)

The *first step* to creating a sustainable gifting experience is understanding the importance of sustainable gifting and why it matters. This means understanding the problems we face.

Our Current Situation

In 2021, tech company Optoro, a reverse logistics tech company, predicted that $120 billion in goods would be returned between Thanksgiving and January. Meagan Knowlton, Director of Sustainability for the company, said, "If returns aren't processed quickly, they take up tremendous space in warehouses and slow down a retailer's ability to fulfill forward deliveries."

Think about it - we are throwing the distribution gearshift in reverse! We purchase unnecessary products not meant to re-enter the market, then return them, mostly unaware of the aftermath that thwarts our forward progress. Imagine driving in rush hour traffic every day for many hours. Now imagine you and everyone else on the highway must drive in *reverse*. On your way to work, traffic moves forward. But in the evening, traffic moves forward but with everyone driving their vehicles in reverse. You would feel frustrated, helpless, stuck, doubtful, possibly insecure, and perhaps even hopeless. That is what reverse logistics is like - a traffic jam of stuff where nothing moves in a timely fashion. Sadly, large companies know what the average consumer does not - the majority of returned products will never get back to their original destination. It's just not good business. Here are some facts to consider:

WHEN DO CONSUMERS PLAN ON RETURNING UNWANTED GIFTS?

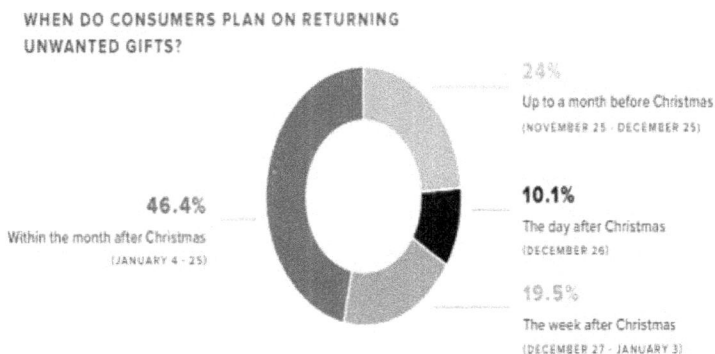

24%
Up to a month before Christmas
(NOVEMBER 25 - DECEMBER 25)

10.1%
The day after Christmas
(DECEMBER 26)

19.5%
The week after Christmas
(DECEMBER 27 - JANUARY 3)

46.4%
Within the month after Christmas
(JANUARY 4 - 25)

- In 2020, overall product returns totaled $428 billion.

- In 2020, 80% of customers planned to do the bulk of their holiday shopping online. This number is expected to increase annually as consumers rely on the convenience and endless selection that shopping online provides.

- Optoro says that more sales typically translate into more returns, and those returns are hitting high-growth retailers more and more.

- Free returns entice customers to feel comfortable enough to make a purchase.

- The gift-giving mentality of "if they don't like it,

they can just return it" is not sustainable.

- Getting the purchased item back on the shelf to resell is far from "free."

- Costs are accrued for retailers in customer service, pick-up and delivery, warehousing, and processing.

- Further revenue is lost from liquidating goods and reselling them at deep discounts - sometimes only ten cents on the dollar.

- These costs might seem irrelevant, but all of these costs are recycled and factored into the ever-increasing price of goods and services.

- Returning one item can cost as much as 66% of the price of that item.

- If a company is already facing the high costs of supply chain chaos, sometimes returns aren't worth their trouble.

- Due to the high costs making most returns fiscally unfeasible, some retailers will tell a dissatisfied customer to keep or donate the item.

These practices have resulted in an uptick in fraudulent returns at a rate of about 6%. We call this *Cyber Shoplifting*, a new scheme that forces businesses to pass costs onto the customer. Navar, a return logistics company, says 75% of typical consumers and up to 90% of VIP customers (brand loyalists) have been told to keep an unwanted item. Amazon, Walmart, Target, Wayfair, Chewy, Wish, Kohl's, and Shein were businesses commonly cited in Navar's survey. Cyber Shoplifting will increase as online shoppers realize which companies provide refunds without asking for the product's return. This will undoubtedly cost us all.

88% of consumers believe that returns go right back on the shelf to be resold to the next consumer.

This belief is false.

Let's take Amazon as an example. Making a return to Amazon couldn't be easier: get a return code and drop it off at your local Kohl's or UPS store, and that's it...out of sight, out of mind. But what happens next?

The goods returned to warehouses generate almost 6 billion pounds of landfill waste and an additional 16 million metric tons of CO_2 emissions. That is equal to the non-gifting waste 3.3 million Americans produce over the course of a year. Returns are expensive to process as well. Amazon would have to go through multiple steps to get that return back to the original seller, which is costly and time-consuming. For these reasons, sellers usually opt for disposal. The unwanted item's final destination is most often the landfill.

"So, you think that your returned gift goes back on the shelf to be resold? Not so much. While this does happen, especially in brick-and-mortar stores, this is the exception and not the norm. Many retailers don't allow previously opened items to be put back on the shelves as new...especially beauty products. These products are typically destroyed or burned, neither method being good for the environment. Many retailers find it easier and cheaper to destroy the rejected item rather than make the effort to repackage and restock. What this turns into is about 5 billion pounds of retail returns being dumped in landfills. Add into that the cost of transporting these items to the landfill, and you have an additional 15 - 16 million metric tons of CO_2 being released into the atmosphere." (NBC News)

Optoro estimates that 5 billion tons of returns end up in landfills annually. This is not the packaging and waste; it's <u>only</u> the returned product. That's the equivalent of 5,600 fully-loaded Boeing 747s!

Many Americans, especially millennials, shop with the return policy in mind, thereby pre-planning for the return and preservation of their capital. A key driver in our purchasing decisions as Americans is "can I get my money back" vs. "is this the right product for me to purchase?" Time spent pre-planning around the return policy could be better spent pre-planning for the perfect purchase. By planning, asking the right questions, being okay with the answers, and shopping according to the information we discover versus our own ideas, we shift from "I hope they like this gift" to "I know they will love this gift. I know they will use this gift." The following illustration shows how return policies contribute to lazy gifting.

Returned Gifts – A Serious Concern

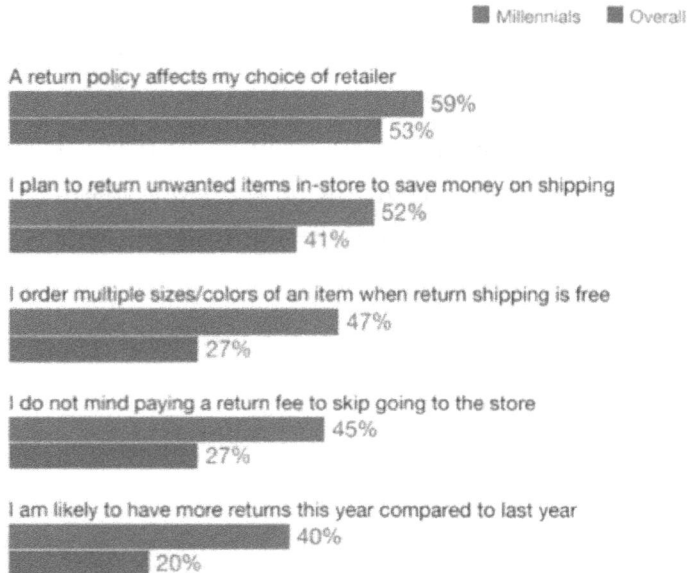

■ Millennials   ■ Overall

A return policy affects my choice of retailer
59%
53%

I plan to return unwanted items in-store to save money on shipping
52%
41%

I order multiple sizes/colors of an item when return shipping is free
47%
27%

I do not mind paying a return fee to skip going to the store
45%
27%

I am likely to have more returns this year compared to last year
40%
20%

•According to the PWC report on holiday shopping in 2020, the millennial (25-38 years) are hyper-focused on return policies.
• More than half (55%) of Americans said they planned on returning unwanted holiday gifts within a month of receiving them, according to a survey published by the National Retail Federation.
• When it comes to buying presents, half of Americans want a simple return policy. Retailers are now using free delivery and returns as a strategic differentiator.
• In addition, the ease of Omni channel returns (i.e., buy digitally, return in-store) is increasing the number of unused gifts returned.

At Optoro, CEO Tobin Moore said companies typically see their returns pile up in warehouses before getting rid of them quarterly or twice a year. "They might liquidate them for pennies on the dollar or even potentially destroy them," he told CBS News correspondent Janet Shamlian, who visited a massive Optoro warehouse outside Nashville, Tennessee. The amount of returned merchandise that ends up in landfills every year is enough to fill 23 million refrigerators or 6,400 Boeing 747s, according to Optoro and the Environmental Capital Group. Optoro's Nashville-area facility is one of three dozen used by the company to process merchandise for sellers like American Eagle, Target, Bed Bath and Beyond, and others. Workers use Optoro's software to catalog the inventory, refund the customer, and relist the product for a new sale. The two following illustrations explain what happens to unwanted gifts and help us understand why purchasing the right gift the first time is so important.

Returns are expensive to process as well. Amazon would have to go through multiple steps to get that return back to the original seller, which is costly and time-consuming. For these reasons, sellers usually opt for disposal. The unwanted item's final destination is most often the landfill.

Where Do The Returned Gifts Go?

Unwanted Gifts Breakdown

Clothing/
Accessories
43%

Household
Items
20%

Cosmetics and
Fragrances
12%

Food and/or Drink
4%

Technology
5%

Music
4%

Literature
8%

Where The Unwanted Gifts Go

31%   31%   20%   7%   4%   4%

● KEEP THEM ● GIVE TO SOMEONE ● EXCHANGE ● SELL ● GIVE THEM BACK

● THROW THEM AWAY

Where Do The Returned Gifts Go?

There are two likely outcomes that can be faced by returned gifts:

Returned gifts

They are resold

- There is a whole industry devoted to helping brands monetize returned goods that cannot be resold through the brand's own channels.

- One company, called B-Stock, is a marketplace for returned, excess, or liquidated goods.

- Companies such as Amazon, Target, Costco, and Home Depot ship returned goods to B-Stock, where other companies or individuals will buy them.

- The buyers buy in bulk and sell on platforms like Poshmark, TheRealReal and eBay.

They go to landfills

- Optoro estimates that 5 billion tons of returns end up annually in landfills.

- That's 5,600 fully loaded Boeing 747s.

- Companies use the earth's precious resources—water-intensive cotton, oil-based plastic, metals—then emit greenhouse gases to transport them to factories around the world, where they're turned into products.

- Then, at the end of that long journey, a significant proportion of those goods will end up in a customer's house for a few days only to be thrown into a landfill.

Points to Ponder

● The sustainable gifting experience saves paper, plastic, cardboard, and other packaging materials that go to waste.

● The sustainable gifting experience saves the planet's resources wasted by manufacturing unwanted gifts.

● The sustainable gifting experience saves maintenance costs and fuel used for trucks, trains, ships, airplanes, and other delivery vehicles.

● The sustainable gifting experience reduces emissions of greenhouse gasses, improves air quality and water supply, and reduces the spread of disease.

● 5.8 billion pounds of returned inventory end up in landfills each year.

● The shipping process emits 16 million metric tons of carbon monoxide annually.

● E-commerce or online shopping produces 14% more waste than in-store shopping.

● In the first few days of January 2021, 8.75 million packages were returned. Most went to landfills.

CHAPTER TWO

The Psychology of Gifting

"Here we are, the most clever species ever to have lived. So how is it we can destroy the only planet we have?"

- Dr. Jane Goodall, Scientist and Activist

"We've been unconsciously disempowering people by giving them beliefs that take away their power."

- Bruce Lipton, Ph.D. – Author, Stem Cell Biologist

The *second step* in creating a sustainable gifting experience is understanding why we do what we do so that we can change our behavior. Until we internalize the why, we will not see value, and if we do not see value, we will not evolve.

To Challenge the Mindset of Gifting, We Must Evolve

To successfully adapt from our previous ideas of what gifting should look like into what gifting must become; to remain an enjoyable and sustainable experience for over 7 Billion people, we must decide to modify our behavior. The Earth demands an evolution of the gifting ritual. It might be fun for us at the moment, while the aftermath is anything but. The ability to decide to evolve will become easier over time. One, because the planet's screams will become increasingly louder until we have no choice except to adapt. Our desire is that we can make this almost-painless shift without suffering through so much more loss of our planet's sustenance. Instead, we can intelligently adjust our behaviors with sustainable practices instead of being forced to do so. Our planet has relentlessly sustained us, and now we must revive it and preserve its ability to provide for all our needs.

To make the shift toward sustainable gifting experiences, our old beliefs need to evolve. Here are what we call, The 10 Understandings. These are serious points to ponder and take into consideration when we shop.

The 10 Understandings

1. **We have the belief that anything is disposable when, actually, no "thing" is disposable.** We need to trash this belief and understand it differently. Whatever you choose to buy is yours forever. That product and all its components belong to you because you took ownership and responsibility for the item when you purchased it. That product required labor, mining, harvesting, gathering, cleaning, design, manufacturing, packaging, shipping, warehouse storage, and distribution. Wherever the plastic, nylon, glitter, paper, tape, foliage, leather, glass, rubber, metal, and the gift ends up, wherever the components migrate to (ocean, street, landfill, our lungs) – that's on you. When we buy a gift now, we should acknowledge our participation in acquiring it, our responsibility in giving it, and the likelihood of the gift ending up in a landfill.

2. **Convenience can't be more important than the health of our planet.** The convenience mindset is wreaking havoc on the health of Americans and people around the globe that adopt US habits. And convenience is wreaking havoc on our planet. We feel entitled to the easiest, fastest, most instantaneous result. Consider all

the energy and resources required to manufacture items we might enjoy the luxury of using just a few times. We can do better by allowing our mindset to evolve, which can be easy and painless. We can choose to see and not look away, and become fulfilled in contributing to our planet's long-term health in lieu of our temporary convenience.

3. **We need to stop believing that people love everything we buy them or that they will make use of our gifts.** Don't believe the hype. An unhappy recipient is unlikely to disclose their true opinions about anything you buy them. They may feel embarrassed for you because you do not even know them well enough to be buying them a gift in the first place. So not only can the gifter feel uncertainty during the gifting experience, but the recipient can also feel frustration, guilt, shame, or embarrassment. No one ever wants to utter the words, *I hate this sweater* even though they are thinking, *you could have kept that.* We've been taught to have etiquette and to show gratitude. After all, it's the thought that counts." But if this monstrous situation is where we find ourselves because it's the thought that counts, as we evolve, we must think better thoughts.

4. **There is a distortion between what we can procure and what we actually have the desire and capacity to use.** Like a buffet, endless choices stretch out before our eyes: colors, patterns, sizes, fabrics, design, trends, flavors, scents, foods, textures, offers, deals, music,

books, self-help, and nostalgia. And like at a buffet, we can only consume so much. The buffet can be lined with all of your favorite foods, but there is still no way you can eat or even taste them all. It is not possible. Nevertheless, guests heap their plates and return for more, even when they know their waistline is already bursting. When we left food on our plates as children, our father used to say, "your eyes are bigger than your stomach." When it comes to acquiring, purchasing, and gifting, it is natural to want what you see. Our evolved thinking must override what the eyes trick our minds into believing we can consume. It's time to adopt a rationale of maturity and preservation, for higher thinking and expectations from ourselves.

5. **Decision fatigue is real.** Studies show that the more choices we make in a day, the more likely we will run out of steam. It is called decision fatigue. Having too many options leads to feeling overwhelmed, causing people to either make bad choices or shut down and do nothing. On the other hand, routines limit the number of decisions you have to make each day, increasing your odds of doing the right thing. Real-life examples of this have been described in studies. For instance, in 2011, Shai Danziger and Liora Avnaim-Pesso of Ben Gurion University and Johnathan Levav of Columbia University studied the various factors affecting the probability that Israeli prisoners who were going before a judge for a parole hearing would be set free. After analyzing over 1,100 decisions over the course of a year, the researchers

found that when it was time to decide if a prisoner should be granted parole, it wasn't the crime committed, the length of the sentence, or the ethnicity of the offender that determined the prisoner's future. Instead, the biggest influence seemed to be *the time of day the prisoner stood in front of the judge.* The prisoners who went to court later in the day were less likely to be released on parole than those who had morning appearances. The judges were not intentionally mistreating prisoners; they were actually experiencing decision fatigue. I shared this quick story with you because we are totally inundated with constant information. Even when we are not cognizant that we are making choices, many times, we are. Numerous options are embedded in comparison shopping, searching for the right gift, and deciding who to buy for. Every search and click presents more choices and countless mini-decisions, which wear us down. So when is the best time to go to a doctor's appointment? Morning. The best time to interview for a job? Morning. The best time to shop? You guessed it. *Morning.*

6. **We may be living vicariously through one another's experiences or helping others live vicariously through ours.** How often have you taken a trip or vacation and felt compelled to bring back a trinket for your family or friends? You want to share the joy and adventure of your experience with those who are not traveling with you. And you find yourself spending brain power thinking about what someone else wants who is not even on the trip. Do you really believe the

overpriced, generic t-shirt with the turtle is the *perfect* gift? Perhaps it is, but for most, it isn't. Too often, it is easy to get lost in the idea that we ought to dole out gifts *from* our traveling experiences. If souvenirs really are your thing, make them the best gifts by choosing the ones that will be loved and wanted.

7. **We may have developed the inability to distinguish between outside influencers' values and our own desires.** I have a colleague who I "think tank" with. Many times I've "introduced" a great idea to him. He sits and listens patiently. Then later, he'll say, ``uh, you know I brought this idea to you about a month ago, right?" I used to argue mildly until I realized he was right. And we were both doing it. We work so closely together on such a broad range of tasks and projects that we lose track of where ideas begin. This also happens as we grow up in our own societies and micro-communities, making it challenging to distinguish our parents' desires from our own. In school, as students, we may have trouble understanding our own truth and what makes us happy due to being exposed to everything everyone wants or says we should have. We can easily transplant our inability to distinguish our desires by relinquishing our *decision obscurities*. We do this by becoming crystal clear about what we want and paying close attention to what others want. This is why it is good to get to know those we buy for and that those who care for us get to know us as well. Knowing exactly *what* to buy is truly the gift that keeps on giving.

8. **We may believe we can buy others' life experiences by accumulating what they have.** Many people really do want to keep up with the Joneses or the Kardashians because we tend to want what others have and covet what we see every day. Their lives appear to be fuller, well-lived, extravagant, exciting, and beautiful. Awe surrounds us as we admire their possessions, opportunities, variety, and access to the world. We are so busy receiving information about who we should be that many of us forget who we truly are. Media and those with means help us discover otherwise invisible things on the world menu, and we love the *things* they show us. If you are not a Kardashian, then you may not have considered the work that goes into being one: early mornings, being away from home and family, exercise, lack of anonymity, and dealing with the haters. It is common to dream and wish for what others have, but we rarely understand what is <u>required </u>to get what they have <u>acquired</u>. We cannot buy our way into being anyone else, no matter what we spend or how we act. Sacrificing financial resources in an attempt to emulate others who are far outside your family's economic threshold is a recipe for disaster. It only promulgates the harsh reality that no amount of gifting can guarantee our sense of worthiness. While admiring beauty and talent is natural and normal, so is supporting those whose values align most with ours.

9. **Surprise is a desire.** Successfully surprising others is a learned aspiration, but creating surprises within the

gifting experience may no longer be sustainable. Remember what Santa does. He checks his list, and he checks it twice. Santa systematically delights and pleases. He does not surprise. He is bringing that little boy and girl precisely what they asked for. Surprises can be wonderful and magical for children and lovely for adults. Evolved mindset asks that we don't always seek the surprise experience at the costly demise of the planet. Be smart.

10. **To create the necessary disruption in our collective consciousness, we must teach our small children a new way of gifting.** Teaching kids new systems to care for self, family, community, and our planet before age seven will be the game changer in solving our reverse logistics dilemma. When we teach children, they teach others and remind us of what we taught them. They do it all the time. If we teach children how to contribute to sustainable gifting experiences when they are very young, we will wire their brains for success and for the reproduction of that experience. They will tether to the task. Children will learn, participate in, and value the simplicity of sustainable gifting because they impact the type of planet they inherit. They will become the "show how" to our "know-how."

Gifting Can Make Us Feel Better About our Past

Seth Godin said, "Black Friday is a media trap, an orchestrated mass hallucination based on herd dynamics and the media cycle." Jacques Cousteau pointed towards overconsumption and overpopulation as underlying contributors to the environmental problems we face today, and David Foreman went further to say that humans have actually *become* a disease. There are mountains of research proving our species' negative impact on our planet. And while we believe in their work and believe there are truths in each of their perspectives, we are careful to align the ideas of this book with the one choice we can make to lessen our negative impact: conscious, sustainable gifting with *zero* returns. I believe that when we have the freedom to make our own choices, then choose to make the right ones, the ones that can have immense ripple effects – that is empowering. Making the right choice and being able to witness the life-changing results in our own lifetimes – that is magical.

Again, this book is not about tearing down the drivers of consumption or berating capitalism. This message is not about telling people to stop buying goods or to stop manufacturing their products to sell. And we are not trying to talk people out of the ritual and customs of shopping and the adrenaline rush that often accompanies scoring the perfect gift! This message is about recognizing the choices we make and how to refine these choices so we can stop harming the planet with our lack of understanding and focus. And one way to pull focus on our actions is to get to the root of the matter. Why do we buy so much? Why do we buy so wrong? Why do we purchase beyond what can be joyfully, meaningfully, and fully managed or consumed? How did the idea that *more is better* become a part of the gift exchange ritual?

Most people do not act, buy, or invest in anything unless there is something in it for them – a payoff, a reward, or a return on their investment. So the root of the matter is that we buy gifts because we are receiving something in return, like a better feeling of wholeness, the joy of reliving our childhoods, or the ability to do for our children and families what our parents could not do. We often comfort our parents, show our love, and honor them by gifting. We give in homage, tradition, guilt, duty, habit, ego, *and* in generosity.

Gifting Can Appear to Lift our Self-Worth

Little House on the Prairie was an older long-running television series that shared the lives and challenges of an early pioneer family. You may have heard of it. Their gifts were singular - one dress or a hair bow, a hairbrush, a pair of socks, a perfectly pressed shirt, or an apron wrapped in brown kraft paper tied with a piece of twine. Each gift was received and appreciated with the same great love with which it was given. They recognized the cost and labor it took to produce their gift, making them love it and cherish it even more. This story, the one of a family surviving, working hard, and raising their children on a very strict budget, is one of the leading psychological reasons we overbuy during holidays.

There is a pain that emanates from the activities surrounding survival and living hand to mouth, paycheck to paycheck. Children who grow up without the clothes and toys their friends' families can afford can store this disappointment, causing them to vow that their own children will never go without. Their children will have the best Christmases. They will have birthday parties every year. They will have everything the parents didn't. They will have *more* than enough. They will not have to suffer. They will not feel worthless or insufficient. They will go to the best schools, wear the best clothes, and their children will not have to feel less than, or undeserving. *Their* children will not be ridiculed about their clothing or appearance. Their children will have all the snacks and tasty treats their tummies can hold.

Seeing those gifts wrapped and situated under the family Christmas tree becomes a satisfying accomplishment that sometimes speaks to both the parent's pain and ego. The gifts the parents provide are more for them and healing their inner child than for the children they seek to spare from feelings of inadequacy. By over-gifting, we are trying to protect our children from ever having to feel the lack we felt. We often hear parents say, "I want better for my children. I don't want them to struggle the way I did." This psychology weaves together countless stories to support all the reasons why people give gifts.

We Can Feel Obligated to Honor Traditions That No Longer Serve Us

We often feel obligated to honor family traditions. Holidays continue to be a magical time of assembling ourselves with those we care about, whether near or far. Homes are bursting with games, rituals, baking, crafts, family photos, travel, hustle and bustle, pretty colors, and mesmerizing lights. Music and fragrances embed themselves into our memories and create mental videos we will remember and feel forever. Most of us can recall our youthful happiness and comfort with just one whiff of a recipe or a few bars of a melody.

Even with all the beauty of the holidays, threads of insecurity sewn alongside these experiences manufacture stress and raise concerns during the holidays. As we grow older, we learn to give based on our relationships with ourselves, our family, our community, and our world. We learn how to give by how people react to us. We feed on feedback and learn to seek particular reactions that validate our decisions. In the hunt for the right reaction or response, we over give and pour out lavishly so we can feel loved, accepted, obedient, or responsible as we perform the rituals we've learned. We do this whether we want to or not, whether we can afford it or not, and our ego lets us and roots us on. We have been trained to create elements of surprise, shop for multiple gifts for one person, and to create experiences we believe to be important, but those good deeds may not even have the effect we're searching for. Perhaps a shift in our mindset might be just what the doctor really ordered.

We have permission to make our choices differently, authentically, lovingly, and thoughtfully to extend the health of our planet. Let's do that, beginning now.

CHAPTER THREE

The Donum App

"Adults keep saying we owe it to the young people to give them hope, but I don't want your hope. I don't want you to be hopeful. I want you to panic. I want you to feel the fear I feel every day. I want you to act. I want you to act as you would in a crisis. I want you to act as if the house is on fire because it is."

– Greta Thunberg, Swedish Environmental Activist

"Oxfam examined 10 of the world's worst climate hotspots, afflicted by drought, floods, severe storms, and other extreme weather, and found their rates of extreme hunger had more than doubled in the past six years."

– The Guardian

"Climate change is real, and it is happening right now."

– Leonardo DeCaprio, Actor and Environmental Activist

The *third step* in creating a sustainable gifting experience is identifying actions and tools that will allow us to change most effectively. In today's culture, that means easily, quickly, and non-invasively.

It might be folklore, but Santa got it right. For one, he asks the kids exactly what they want. Then he asks them if they have been naughty or nice. Because if you're on the naughty list, you can forget it. He is not about to waste his time in supersonic flight, placing himself and his reindeer at risk for someone who doesn't care enough to behave themselves. Meaning you do not have to buy gifts for everyone just to be nice or to keep up appearances. If someone doesn't enhance or enrich your life in some way, you have permission to refrain from obligatory gifting.

Then here's the genius. He hand delivers each gift, and there is no way to return them. The North Pole does not receive gift returns. The North Pole doesn't employ a reverse logistics engineering firm to orchestrate gift returns, because there is no need to. He knows sizes, colors, brands, allergies, addresses, and whether you use an android or an iPhone. Santa does his homework. That's what he spends the remainder of the year doing: supervising elves, reading and cataloging gift requests, conducting research, and planning his route. Duh.

Santa would never bring a child a gift they didn't ask for. That's why he makes his list and checks it *twice*. We imagined what Santa would think about all of this. Misgifting, mass gifting, gifting without intel, reverse logistics. When we interviewed Santa, he said he didn't understand why everyone seemed to think that he needed their help. He said that we took what was made to spread joy to children throughout the world and somehow began to include every adult we could imagine. He explained that although gifting is for everyone, the surprise and magic were truly intended for the children. He went on to explain that even though it gives him great joy to see others spreading Christmas cheer, the surprise aspect is costing us all dearly.

See, when he gives a gift, the children are not as surprised as they are overjoyed and delighted. Why is that? Because they already know what they are going to get. They know Santa has their backs. They do their part in sharing the true desire of their hearts. Then he does his part. He said that most kids truly only want one or two things and that it is highly unlikely that a child will enjoy more gifts than that. This is due to the fact that humans, including little humans, gravitate towards their favorites, and typically superfluous gifts fade into the background. He asked us about our closets and what percentage of the clothes in them, we would say were our favorites. Seeing us struggle with this question, he broke it down. "What did you wear last week? And what did you wear this week?"

"You are going to wear your favorite clothes and ignore the others. You are going to wear your favorite jewelry and your most comfortable shoes. You tune into your favorite channels. You visit your favorite restaurants. Get it? It's easy. Kids are just like that. Everyone returns to the aspects and tools in their lives that give them the greatest comfort and joy." We gained a lot of clarity from our conversation, and his philosophy, once again, illuminated quality over quantity, buying goods that will last versus being temporary, and truly buying gifts kids - both big and small - will love, use, and cherish.

Santa never intended for us to pump up the volume on gifting to the extent that surprising children would write them a check their future can't cash – that gifts now would cost them air quality, polar bears, and even put Santa's North Pole digs in jeopardy as the ice melts around Mrs. Santa's welcome mat.

In 2019, Americans spent over one trillion dollars on Christmas. The increased demand has greatly challenged Santa's responsibility to deeply understand children's desires. He credits his partners, especially Amazon, Walmart, Target, and other big retailers, as catalysts in helping to cover the globe with gifts for everyone. He said these relationships have enhanced his omnipresence. "But," he went on, "neither the presence nor the *presents* seem worth the price. They just don't."

We noted Santa's demeanor as we chatted, and he grew more thoughtful, bowing his tilted head as he remembered simpler days. He explained how children are so self-aware that they know exactly what they want. They know what makes them happy. We just tend not to believe them. We tend to believe that more is more and that more stuff equates to more happiness, but that's just not true.

Santa campaigns in person. He gets up close and personal with his children and asks two very important questions. Have you been good? And what do you want for Christmas? We should be that wise. The great thing is that it is not too late for us to reshape our thinking, expectations, and habits surrounding gifting. When we collectively accomplish this, sustainable gifting will become an art and expression of understanding our collective genius. The main two reasons we have collectively brought gift-giving to a level that is unsustainable for our planet is that we have not evolved in our beliefs of what gifting means. We refuse to color within the lines and obey the laws of nature, and the truth of what nature can bear.

(Tracey)

I am old enough to remember the two-lane roads in my hometown. Over the years, I witnessed those narrow roads grow to four lanes. I saw Interstate 88 broaden from four lanes to eight. Every time I return home, there are changes. Many widened roads. New highway exits where there weren't any. New toll booths to pay for all the improvements. When navigating those newer roads, I have a choice. I can fall in line with the new lanes and respect the dotted lines that keep all drivers safely separated and organized into our own lanes. Or I can live in the past and act like the changes never happened.

I can drive the roads as I remember them or as they are now. If I insist on living in the past and swerving all over the road, driving down the middle of two lanes because that is where I remember the road being, my actions will cause trouble for me and everyone else. And if I persist, eventually, I will be pulled over and ticketed, hurt, killed, or do reckless damage to someone else. Regardless of what happens, the fact is something is going to happen to stop my behavior, and I must pay the price for insisting on living in yesteryear. Can you imagine how the conversation would go with the police officer?

Officer: "Ma'am, do you know why I stopped you?"

Me: "Nope."

Officer: "Well, you were driving down the middle of two lanes. Didn't you hear the other drivers honking at you to move over?"

Me: "I heard them. I didn't know they were honking at me."

Officer: "Do you normally drive down the middle of the street?"

Me: "No, but I remember this being a two-lane road. So, I was just driving where the old lanes used to be."

Officer: "Have you been drinking, ma'am?"

Me: "No. I just don't want to change."

The point is this. We can continue to engage in the unsustainable and reckless behavior of mindlessly appealing to our own desires and sometimes egocentric methods of gifting, but there is a collective cost we all must pay. We are already doing so.

The Solution

The Donum App is designed to prevent returns and to provide a customized and sustainable gifting experience every time. Will packages get lost? Yes. Will products not work properly, possibly arrive damaged, or in the very rare event, not fit? Yes, but not nearly to the degree we were at in 2021. The app minimizes misgifting by capturing all the information about the recipient's gifting philosophy and preferences: favorite colors, scents, allergies, brands, restaurants, and foods. The Donum app allows you to select exactly what you truly want and need from this huge world of choices. You can keep track of all the desires of your heart – forever. Then, you can share your profile with those in your tribe, so everyone can mutually and responsibly gift with laser accuracy. Now people can stop buying you shit you don't want. And you can stop buying shit your tribe doesn't want. This app is Santa's new right-hand man.

Reasons to Use the Donum App

- You will get what you really want.

- You will give others what they really want.

- Keep a lifelong wish list that changes as your preferences shift.

- You can include all shopping categories: kids, home, garden & outdoors, technology, charities, foods and beverages, everyday items, back to school, electronics, hobbies, self-care, beauty, and travel.

- Take the guesswork out of the gifting experience.

- Take the emotions and social pressure out of gifting.

- Easily choose gifts in any price range without the guilt of underspending or overspending.

- Prevent the return of unwanted gifts.

- Eliminate worry about over or under-spending.

- Increase joy and pleasure in the gifting process.

- Save valuable time, travel, and resources for you, others, and the planet, including raw materials, non-renewable natural resources, fuel, and energy.

- Help prevent price increases due to the burden reverse logistics places on distribution channels.

Sustainable gifting with Donum may mean challenging our outdated beliefs, customs, or traditions that no longer transfer true meaning. This is as simple as asking ourselves why we are doing what we are doing. You may always buy fruitcakes as a tradition, but you know full well that no one is eating the fruitcakes. They are sitting on kitchen counters and dining tables, hardening with each passing day. Does gifting fruitcakes serve you and others? Or is there a more useful way you can adapt to a more modern and sustainable gifting experience?

Teaching our Children the Art of Sustainable Gifting

Modernizing the gifting experience means teaching our children about gifting and the costs we all will incur to provide meaningful and nourishing gifts to one another during celebrated life events and holidays. It is crucial that we begin to hardwire our children's thoughts with self-discipline, self-awareness, and the spirit of *enoughness*. As human beings, many times, we want most everything we see, but we cannot use everything we have. There are hundreds of delicious foods and restaurants, but if you place an entree on my table from every restaurant we like, it does not matter how much we like the food or desire the food, we simply cannot eat it all. We can't even taste it all; It is impossible, and waste is guaranteed. This is not a hypothesis. This is a fact. In the same way, we have to practice gifting within a realm of *enoughness* and teach our children that the space of *enoughness* is not only healthy, it is a loving gesture to themselves, their community, and the world.

Surprises are expensive: paper, plastic, fabric, metallic, wrapping, cardboard, bows, labels, plastic, precious and non-precious metals, lumber, plants, chemicals, fossil fuels, labor, air-truck-boat-train transport, gasses, glass, labor, and water. It is a fact that as inhabitants of Earth, we must use its resources to survive, thrive, and achieve a semblance of comfort. It is a fact that one day the Earth will die – just like we will. Over time, our bodies will change and show wear and age. Most humans prioritize the care of their bodies to enjoy health and longevity. To others, the care of their bodies is not a priority. The Earth is like our bodies, except that the Earth is used by all of us, and its preservation is all of our responsibilities. We know we need the planet. But how we use the planet is improvable.

You have the right to eat whatever you want, go wherever you want, live wherever you want, and be whatever you want – however you want. These immense freedoms have impacted the planet. We realize it is impossible to get everyone to do one thing at the same time, support one common mission, or even care about one thing. However, the world can and will change if enough people choose to modernize their thinking towards more thoughtful shopping, common sense purchasing, and targeted gift buying.

Know what the gift recipient desires, how they live, their

gifting awareness, and philosophy. Just because you love something does not mean someone you love will love it. They might love your gesture. They might like the gift. They might think it is clever, but that does not mean they will ever use it. This one assumption lies at the heart of irresponsible gifting or *misgifting*. We assume colors, patterns, and styles. We estimate sizes. We casually buy thinking, "hey if they don't like it, they can return it." Or "I'll just get both sizes, and they can return the one that doesn't fit." What?

(Tracey)

Every year for the past 15 years, I have shipped Portillo's Hot Dogs from Chicago, IL, to my son, Rod, for his birthday, wherever he was living in the world at the time. The box comes with hot dogs, buns, mustard, onion, tomato, and peppers. I ship them because he grew up eating them and because he loves them and because I have seen him wolf them down with such joy and reckless abandonment throughout his childhood and because of the nostalgia and the good times and good feelings surrounding all of our rainy Saturdays in Portillo's restaurant long ago. I ship them because it is convenient. It is super fun for him to get the cooler, which he repurposes, and because he shares them with his friends. So good people, when his birthday comes around every year at the same exact time, I do not have to ponder, search, agonize, or question! I just go online and place the order. I have a 100% no-return rate. I have a 100% satisfaction rate. His joy is palpable. I retain my title as the best mom in the entire universe. Repeat. That is how sustainable gifting is done. The gift does not have to be sustainable in and of itself; it is the purchaser who determines whether the gifting experience is sustainable or not.

So, I don't factor in his cholesterol, whether he's grown too old for hot dogs, or if onlookers disapprove because the 17th annual box is beyond the gifting quota. I have a runaway hit on my hands! There is zero angst in my process. It's not that expensive, and if he ever goes vegan, I will figure it out! What I am saying is to know your people. Take the guesswork out of gifting and save the planet while easily gifting. The joy of giving this gift is his delight. Remember, that is what Santa does. His goal is not to surprise. His goal is to delight. If you want to delight and create a sustainable gifting experience, simply find out what your peeps want. We've included a worksheet on page 80 that will help you get to know those for whom you buy. The Donum gifting app makes it easy for us to get to know one another so we can buy gifts that are guaranteed to be loved. That is the whole point, and that creates a win for you, the recipient, and the planet.

Even if they like it doesn't mean they will use it. This is so important to remember. The reason for this is that everyone has their own brands they're particular about. We like certain colors and hues within those colors. We prefer certain fabrics – the feel, texture, sheen, and drape, and how the fabric envelops us. So while we may "like" a gift, it does not mean it will make it into our regular rotation. We all have brand preferences, and a gift can be similar to what we like but not exactly what we want. For example, some people like Fishers mixed nuts, while others like Planters or Nuts.com. As people become more mature and self-aware, they know what they like and what they don't like. Trust people to tell you the truth. Then get out of the way, listen, and respond with appropriate gifting behaviors. If you have gifts sitting in someone's home collecting dust, or their seasonal gifts are not being remembered or used, you have not been sustainably gifting.

The Donum app fixes most gifting issues by allowing the user to set their preferences. This single-handedly transforms the gifting game. The app expands upon the Amazon wish list because items from any store can be uploaded to a Donum profile by scanning a product barcode or typing the item's details into the user's list.

The app will display:

- The exact gifts desired

- Sizes, colors, fragrances, allergies, tech preferences (IOS, Android, Google)

- What not to buy

- How much the gift costs

- How the users' gifts are ranked according to desire

- Categories they do not want the shopper to purchase

- Where to buy it

People say, "it's the thought that counts." but it isn't. It's the gift that counts because our misgifting is flooding landfills, not our thoughts. If you are giving a gift, the experience is not about you or what you think. Landfills are overflowing with unwanted items being dumped by reverse logistic warehouses right now because you think you can read minds or you blindly guess what someone prefers and will actually use. And, of course, there are a few people in our lives who we know that well. We know how to buy for them, and that is wonderful, but that is not the norm.

When half of all people who receive gifts at Christmas

are planning to return one or more items, we, as a collective, are not getting it right.

People worry about how much gifts cost. They worry about how much they should spend.

Attempting to select the right gift can cause uncertainty and frustration to the shopper, who, on average, spends over fifteen hours every Christmas searching for gifts. Shoppers ruminate over price, torn between spending too little or too much. Opting for cash or random gift cards could put a band-aid on the issue, but the root problems persist. Obligated gifters pace in front of the wall of cards, unsure of the proper store and dollar amount to send. What do we say or do when we receive a purple sweater when my aunt has never seen me wear purple a day in my life, and we don't want to hurt her feelings, and it is kind of snug? Then there's the flushed feeling of fake smiling and trying to be grateful as we realize that this person really doesn't know us at all—they are giving us the hockey tickets their boss gave them, and we hate hockey (We don't hate hockey, that's just an example.) People worry about how much gifts cost. They worry about how much they should spend. No one wants to be viewed as cheap or one who lacks effort. People wonder, what if they spend more on me than I do on them?

Donum app users will experience less stress in searching

for and possibly affording the desires of others because all users provide a range of items in every price range. From dream gifts to more practical everyday items, users provide invaluable information about themselves that makes the shopper's life easy. Recipients will feel good because they've taken the time to set up a system where their tribe can easily delight them without the worry of waste. Afterall, the recipients pre-selected the gifts that they are 100% satisfied with, preventing gift returns way before they happen. When utilizing the Donum platform, the only reasons anyone should return a gift are quality or performance defects, not because of size, color, design, usefulness, or preference. When an item is purchased on the app, it is marked as purchased. A gifter can purchase an additional item if the recipient desires more than one. Otherwise, the icon remains on the app so the user never loses the data, but since it is marked purchased, they don't have to worry about receiving a duplicate item.

The only person who knows if you are going to love a gift is you. That is why you must tell people what you want and what you do not want. You will also need to keep your app updated with new things you want or update sizes. We should not be buying gifts hoping. Hoping it fits, hoping it's the right color, hoping they like it, or hoping they don't have one just like it. Buying a gift should not require faith or luck— just the facts.

The user can also create a "no-no" list for those who might peruse your app profile for ideas and then buy something 'similar.' You can let people know you prefer they do not buy you clothes or shoes. You can be picky. Part of the responsibility in the sustainable gifting experience model is to prevent others from buying certain things you know you are most likely going to be disappointed with. This requires that we be more direct with articulating our values and purpose in order to create change. Facebook is an awesome social media platform, but it will not help you buy the right gift. Pinterest is a beautiful and rich space to pin and vision board to your heart's content, but it will not teach your friends or family how to choose the specific gifts you're daydreaming about.

The Donum app is a lifelong account of all we love, use, and desire. It is the wedding registry we never have to delete. It is the birthday wish list that grows with us. It is a declaration of what we stand for and what we want out of our gifting experience. The app gives us the power to define the commerce coming into and flowing out of our lives.

CHAPTER FOUR

How to Buy a Gift

"Everything depends on our ability to sustainably inhabit this earth, and true sustainability will require us all to change our way of thinking on how we take from the earth and how we give back."

– Deb Haaland

"Give the public the 'image' of what it thinks it ought to be, or what television commercials or glossy magazine ads have convinced us we ought to be, and we will buy more of the product, become closer to the image, and further from reality."

– Madeleine L'Engle

The _fourth step_ in creating a sustainable gifting experience is to learn how to shop for the recipient. This involves removing your opinions, values, and preferences about what other people want and what's best for their lifestyles. We modernize our behavior by responsibly decreasing the parts of our traditional gifting habits that no longer serve us.

This is hard, but the question must be asked. Do you know how to properly purchase a gift? We mean, really, do you know how to buy a gift; not shop, but _buy_? Is your gift special, thoughtful, useful, and not necessarily always a surprise? Do you know who you are buying for? Are you buying for the right reasons? Do you make purchases out of guilt? When you become exhausted with the hunt, do you just cave in and buy something, thinking, "they can always return it if they don't like it?"

One essential part of modernized and sustainable gifting is saying goodbye to the tradition of surprise adrenaline and the comforting ritual of thoughtful exchange. Gift-giving can evolve as we mature and move from the element of fun and wonder to a less complex, more fulfilling agreement between us and those we care for and who care for us. And to make this transition, we need to know the people in our tribe and what matters to them. Not us, them.

You are the original owner of and responsible party for everything you buy— whether you keep it or not.

Ask people in your life the following questions, which will help you understand what matters to *them*. What their gift philosophies are. What their needs are. What brands they use - from skincare to household products. What do they see as useful? What brands do they enjoy? Consider the following categories, not just what is trending at the moment.

Back to School

Wedding

Anniversaries

Birthdays

Baby Showers

Hobbies

Home

Lawn and Garden

Art, Music, Books

Food

Technology

Travel

The Great Outdoors

Everyday Stuff

Health and Beauty

The more self-aware we can be, the better we can enable others to participate in win-win gift exchanges that put a stop to reverse logistics. Here are a few gifting profiles to help you understand your friends, family, and coworkers. This understanding is invaluable as you strive to purchase gifts that your tribe loves and would never think of returning.

(Tracey)

I think kitchen gadgets are super cool! I also know that no matter how cool they are, I am highly unlikely to use them. However, if you get me a gardening tool or gadget, I will definitely use it. I know I don't like people buying me clothes, but I do think scarves and wraps are very interesting.

By using a gifting profile such as the ones on the following pages, you can zero in on what to buy and what not to buy for your loved ones. The app offers more personalization options, but even this simple questionnaire will help you shop more confidently and sustainably.

Tracey's Gifting Profile

GIFTING PROFILE
WORKSHEET

This easy-to-use worksheet is designed to help save you time, frustration, and anxiety because you are confidently buying something the receiver loves and you will not need to overspend. Have the people you buy for fill this out for you and share a copy of your completed worksheet with the people that buy for you.

BIO

Name	Tracey Lynch
Birthday	Ex: 1/1/1975
Important dates	Ex. Add birthday, anniversary
Preferred sizes (clothes, linens, etc.)	N/A
Allergies/dietary restrictions	None
Dislikes *Include things to never buy for you*	Waste, excessive packaging, things I don't need, items that are highly patterned, strong fragrances, one-use products, items that are not well made, store-bought greeting cards with no personal handwriting inside, aerosol cans, Never buy me clothes, shoes, socks, kitchen gadgets and tools, perfumed lotion, perfume sets.
Gifting philosophy *Your gifting philosophy is how you feel about receiving gifts and can include your values and reasons. This statement helps the gifter get to know you better.*	My gift philosophy is practical and authentic. I enjoy gifts that I can use versus trendy items. I don't like to waste, so sustainable products are appreciated, as well as practical items I use every day. I love social entrepreneurship, so gifts that support causes and local businesses mean a lot to me. I don't need to be surprised. However, I cherish being thought of in a personal and meaningful way.

FAVORITES

Gifts you most like to receive	Jar candles that burn well, incense sticks, cloth napkins, bamboo hand towels, cotton sack towels, glassware, cast iron cookware, Grove cleaning products, shawls, interesting fabrics, global handmade items, books, word art, journals, crystals, tiki torches and oil, coffee, tea, honey, olive oil, spices, cheeses, charcuterie. I also collect white dinnerware, green wreaths, and buddhas.
Brands	Ralph Lauren, Apple (IOS), Level 8, Tumi, Dr. Bronner's, Coach, Marlborough Sauvignon Blanc, Wild Foods
Stores	Chewy.com, Crate and Barrel, Resale shops, Trader Joe's, Restoration Hardware, Hilton Hotels, Boutique Hotels, Nuts.com, Fresh Thyme
Scents	Thymes Frasier Fir, Jasmine, honeysuckle, gardenia, smoky scents, Opium classic parfum, lavender room spray, vanilla, nag champa, apple, tobacco, lemon.
Foods	Japanese, Mexican, Ethiopian
Restaurants	Good sushi, Seasons 52

OTHER

Body, Mind, Soul	Salt cave, massage, reflexology, facial, Dr. Teal's body wash and Epsom salts, dead sea clay, museum tickets, zoo passes, theater tickets, Dr. Joe Dispenza meditations, inspiring literature, a night's stay at a nearby national park.
Things I use every day	Coffee, French press, mushroom powder, turmeric, ashwagandha, vitamins, face wash, moisturizer, goat milk body cream, probiotics, Seventh Day and Method cleaning products, colored sharpies, journal, and notebooks.
Hobbies	Reading, gardening, hiking, documentaries

MY PERFECT...

My perfect gift basket would have	Popcorn, avocados, olive oil, castile soap, incense, candles, wine, local honey, dark chocolate, Epsom salts
My wish list	Snowshoes, Apple watch, sled, nail grinder for my pups

Rod's Gifting Profile

GIFTING PROFILE
WORKSHEET

This easy-to-use worksheet is designed to help save you time, frustration, and anxiety because you are confidently buying something the receiver loves and you will not need to overspend. Have the people you buy for fill this out for you and share a copy of your completed worksheet with the people that buy for you.

BIO

Name	Rod Strozier
Birthday	Ex. 1/1/1992
Important dates	N/A
Preferred sizes (clothes, linens, etc.)	Men's medium shirts and loungewear.
Allergies/dietary restrictions	None
Dislikes include things to never buy for you	I really dislike things that feel fake or are low quality because I want them to last and not contribute to a landfill. I don't like things that I don't love. Never buy me any clothing I didn't say I wanted, jewelry, shoes, gift cards to restaurants.
Gifting philosophy Your gifting philosophy is how you feel about receiving gifts, and can include your values and reasons. This statement helps the gifter get to know you better.	My gifting philosophy is centered around health, spirituality, human revolution, and longevity. I like to receive gifts that expand my way of thinking and challenge me to be a better and stronger person. I am passionate about fitness, the outdoors, off-the-grid living, and food. I truly dislike receiving items I won't use, including gift cards to restaurants. I'm just going to donate it or give it away and neither of us want that.

FAVORITES

Gifts you most like to receive	Books, useful antiques, outdoor and survival tools, cookware, knives, merino wool clothing, camera, and production equipment, tea, coffee, and spices.
Brands	Wild Foods, Ten Thousand, PaleoValley, KettleBell Kings, CK Maceworks, Whoop, Bulletproof, Dr. Bronner's, Vevo
Stores	Butcher Box, REI, Patagonia, Apple, Trader Joes, Thrift and Resale Shops, Co-ops
Scents	Patchouli, Sandalwood, Thieves, Frankincense, LaCoste cologne
Foods	Grass-fed meats, superfoods.
Restaurants	Local farm to table restaurants are my faves!

OTHER

Body, Mind, Soul	Oracle or tarot decks, essential oils, candles, Gold Bond body lotion, books. Dr. Joe Dispenza, Tim Ferris, Shawn Stevenson, and Don Miguel Ruiz are some of my favorite authors.
Things I use every day	Vitamins, tea kettle, French press, face and body wash, kettlebells, gym clothes.
Hobbies	Strength training, archery, reading.

MY PERFECT...

My perfect gift basket would have	Beef and bison jerky, Kombucha, red wine, cheese, chocolate, cured meats, word puzzle books, tarot cards, coffee
My wish list	Camper tent for my truck, Merino wool clothing in light and medium layers, kettlebells 70 pound each

Gifting Profile Worksheet

You can use this questionnaire with those you buy for and share your version with those who buy for you. It will save you time, frustration, and anxiety because you are confidently buying something the receiver loves, and you will not need to overspend.

- What is your gifting philosophy?
- What are your dislikes?
- What are your favorite gifts to receive?
- Never buy me this!
- Sizes
- Favorite Brands/Favorite Stores
- Favorite Scents
- Body, Mind, Soul
- Things I use everyday
- Wish List

GIFTING PROFILE
WORKSHEET

This easy-to-use worksheet is designed to help save you time, frustration, and anxiety because you are confidently buying something the receiver loves and you will not need to overspend. Have the people you buy for fill this out for you and share a copy of your completed worksheet with the people that buy for you.

BIO

Name	
Birthday	
Important dates	
Preferred sizes (clothes, linens, etc.)	
Allergies/dietary restrictions	
Dislikes Include things to never buy for you	
Gifting philosophy Your gifting philosophy is how you feel about receiving gifts, and can include your values and reasons. This statement helps the gifter get to know you better.	

FAVORITES

Gifts you most like to receive	
Brands	
Stores	
Scents	
Foods	
Restaurants	

OTHER

Body, Mind, Soul	
Things I use every day	
Hobbies	

MY PERFECT...

| My perfect gift basket would have | |
| My wish list | |

The only way to know someone will enjoy and appreciate your gift is if they tell you what they want.

Everyone has a list of stuff they could and would use. Whether it's a silicone ice cube tray set, a Malbec you enjoy, a beautiful set of long-stemmed wine glasses, a piece of cookware to add to your set, cushions for your patio furniture, new guest towels, rain boots, throw pillows for your family room, reading glasses you saw in a magazine, a holiday wreath for your front door, stamps, planners, candles.

It can be difficult to find anyone an item that will become a favorite well-used possession. It can also be challenging to relay our feelings about possessions and how we use them in a meaningful way that better enables others to buy gifts that satisfy us. The only way to know someone will enjoy and appreciate your gift is if they tell you what they want. So allow them to tell you. Ask them to tell you. This "allowing" is a two-way street, though. We must be willing to share our gifting philosophy and preferences with those who care for us. Instead of telling them, "I do not want anything," or "please do not buy anything for me," or "I don't need anything," be kind enough to those who desire to show you kindness by sharing a few gift ideas. If people care about you, eventually, they are going to want to buy you something. As we evolve toward a sustainable gifting mentality, it becomes our responsibility to inform others of who we really are and what we really stand for. That is the only way a gift becomes a win for the giver, the recipient, and the planet.

We use the convenience of mail orders and online shipping as ways to fantasy shop, and guess what we *might* like. We are well trained to know we can return whatever we don't like for almost any reason, but the ability to process returns is a quickly growing cancerous growth to our planet. It is a logistics and inventory problem we all pay for. Just like we all pay higher insurance and medical costs because we *share* the cost of chronic diseases such as obesity, heart disease, and diabetes; we also share the increased cost of wasting gifts and returning them in terms of what we pay for goods, shipping, packaging, and distribution.

As we select gifts for ourselves and for others, we will reduce waste significantly if we buy better quality goods. When we choose to adopt the practice of quality ownership, we increase the possibility that the goods we purchase will last a lifetime. By aiming for lifetime ownership, we can better avoid repurchasing experiences. Shop for lifetime warranties to protect your purchase. Consider owning less variety.

It takes months for a merchant to prepare for any holiday, but especially for Christmas. Orders are planned and placed many months in advance. Distribution channels and warehouse strategies are set in place and meticulously followed. This process is how we manage to receive just about anything we desire with accuracy and timeliness. Just remember – all of the logistical planning in the world cannot possibly handle a reversal of those same goods, commencing all at once, converging from all over the world at one time—it is catastrophic, and it can't be fixed with reverse logistics. Warehouses can brace for the storm of influx, but the returns travel like a typhoon, relentlessly sucking from the land and then violently crashing back. The only way to fix it is by changing our minds about gifting and deciding to do a better job.

The Earth is demanding we do better. If your child cries out, saying their tummy hurts, you pay attention. If they have a high fever, you take it seriously because high fevers indicate infection or virus. Something has infiltrated your child's immune system, and you will not sit back without taking action. So this is our time to show concern and collectively take some ER action for our planet's sake and to protect what our children will inherit.

Points to Ponder

- Choose gifts wisely and based on firsthand info from the recipient.

- Gather enough information to make the right choice.

- Focus on the recipient, not on yourself and how you will be perceived.

- Remember charitable giving as an option.

- Do not buy unneeded items for the sake of the gesture.

- Do not assume the recipient will love your gift. Half of all gift recipients immediately plan to return one or more items.

- Use the Donum app to get it right the first time.

- Some enjoy buying souvenirs when traveling. This is a great opportunity to buy unique items such as fabrics, jewelry, carved and handmade goods, and art to gift later on IF you buy for someone who loves these types of things.

CHAPTER FIVE

Sustainable Everyday Gifting Ideas

"It's pretty amazing that our society has reached a point where the effort necessary to extract oil from the ground, ship it to a refinery, turn it into plastic, shape it appropriately, truck it to a store, buy it and bring it home, is considered to be less effort than what it takes to just wash the spoon when you're done with it."

– Unknown

"The world is changed by your example, not by your opinion."

– Paulo Coelho

"...most of the damage we cause to the planet is the result of our own ignorance."

– Yvon Chouinard, Let My People Go Surfing: The Education of a Reluctant Businessman

The _fifth step_ in creating a sustainable gifting experience is to be crystal clear about what your tribe wants, while also communicating your specific desires. Otherwise, you are all shooting in the dark and contributing to landfills full of unwanted gifts.

With the Donum platform, you can keep everyone's likes and dislikes at your fingertips. When you are shopping sales or on vacation, you can confidently scoop up treasures that your people will love, avoiding those "just because" items that they will never use.

We said earlier in this book that we are not campaigning to overthrow the traditions of exchanging gifts or nullify the joys of shopping. This short journey has been about becoming a more thoughtful shopper and learning how to master sustainable gifting since the way we are doing it now is unsustainable. We are learning to infuse our gift-giving with respect for the environment. That is the essence of sustainable shopping. Not just buying items that were made in more sustainable ways but educating ourselves on what we actually should be buying in the first place. By reviewing people's Donum profiles prior to shopping, we can collectively extend the lifespan of our entire planet.

So yes, go ahead and buy the gift – but first, make sure it is just right in the receiver's eyes. Gifting is about the recipient, not about you. Let me repeat that. Their perfect present is not about you. It is not about your tastes or preferences or your ego. The gift is about *them*. We know why. We know what the issue is. We know who this is about. We know when we need to adopt this new consciousness. And we know where.

The Donum app provides the how. But there is a little more "how" we want to talk about. We know that even after you download the app and begin using it with great glee, you will still purchase gifts and shop for your home and personal needs.

This is where you can begin to expand your consciousness further and create a deeper impact from your personal experience.

Gifts are not necessarily meant to be saved. Other than nostalgic gifts such as photographs, restored items from the past, or personalized items, gifts are meant to be used. Even some of these more sentimental items or personalized gifts may have a use. People already know what they want to buy for themselves, a significant other, or a parent/child that might be a keepsake. There is no replacement for a keepsake, but other than that, try to purchase gifts that will be consumed, that have immediate use, and especially gifts that the recipient would buy regardless of whether you did or not.

Here are examples of items people are already purchasing and going to buy anyway—whether you purchase it for them or not. This is the sustainable gifting goldmine.

Gym membership dues

Extend or renew their existing membership

Household cleaning

Identify the brands they love first. Don't buy just anything.

Candles, Home fragrances

A *lovely and luxurious gift for those who partake.*

Beauty and personal items like moisturizer, eye cream, and face wash

Get to know their favorite brands and stick to them. This is useful and thoughtful.

Vitamins, Protein Supplements

These are invaluable and can be a wonderful way to show you care and augment their budget. They will be so excited you paid attention.

Coffee, Tea, Honey

Discover their favorite brands or find out if they are open to surprises. This can be a beautiful, practical, and luxurious gift all in one. These are also great items to buy during travels.

Food

There are seafood, meat, grocery, and specialty foods online. Get to know your audience and buy frozen or well-packaged. Think New Orleans gumbo, Portillo's Hotdogs, Garrett's Popcorn, local free-range meats, ribs, specialty baked goods, and wonderful foods from all over the world.

Gasoline

Anyone who drives can use a gas card, especially useful to those on a strict budget, students, seniors, road warriors, and travelers

Oil Changes/Car Maintenance

Another awesome gift. People tend to put off car maintenance which hurts gas mileage. Find out where they prefer to take their vehicle. Maybe even take it to get serviced for them.

Car Washes

A pack of car washes or a subscription are awesome ways to give a gift that keeps giving throughout the year.

Wine, Beer, and Alcohol

Specialty beers, favorite wines, and alcohol are always thoughtful and welcome to those who enjoy them.

Live Seasonal Wreaths, Garland, Seasonal Doormats

This is a lovely Christmas idea that you can give prior to Christmas and be done with it. Trader Joe's has awesome live greenery every year, many of which can be composted or planted in springtime. Seasonal doormats can be shipped at the same time you mail your Christmas cards.

Gardening Supplies

Pay attention to the gardeners in your life. Gloves, hand tools, seeds, water hoses, natural weed and pesticide products, kneeling pads, and wagons. If you are a gardener, consider gifting homegrown plants in personalized containers.

Collections

Anything to add to an existing collection - like *knives, crystals, dolls, silver, books, and cookware. Who wouldn't love to have an omelet pan added to the cookware set they are collecting?*

Phone & Computer Accessories

Earbuds, headphones, charging pads, iPad or MacBook cases, software

Travel & Luggage

A needed piece of luggage or carry-on, makeup travel bags, ultra-lightweight travel items like jackets, nylon bags, travel pants, travel undies, airfare, contribution to accommodations

Sustainable Products

Cloth napkins, recyclable grocery and wine bags,

Personal kits (reusable straw, reusable chopsticks, napkin, mug, plate), picnic baskets with place settings, salt and pepper shakers, condiment containers, cloth napkins. These are not gifts for everybody, so choose carefully.

Cooler

Fill a cooler with festive drinks and have it all ready to go! Merry Christmas! Great for Father's Day or the Fisherman in your life.

Seasonal

Patio Furniture, portable chairs, umbrellas, and cushion replacements - Shop the end of the season for deep discounts while retailers haul in Back-to-School merchandise!

Back to School

Books, school supplies, bedding, small appliances

Nostalgia

Framed photographs, touchnote cards, personalized photography blankets say so much and are super affordable. Handwritten letters are kind, special, and memorable.

All these categories and more are available on the Donum app so you can identify your favorites. Then, others can thoughtfully, easily, and sustainably shop for you AND so you will know your tribe member's favorite items so you can create a sustainable gifting experience for them.

Just because you can do something

does not mean you should.

and

Just because you can buy something does not mean you should.

We love contributing to the creation and sustainability of jobs and we know that by consuming goods, we create opportunities for our fellow citizens. Someone gets to earn a living developing, designing, manufacturing, packaging, and shipping my products. We are so grateful for the opportunity to be involved in a global society where we are able to secure the things we need when we desire to have them. That is awesome, and I would not change it. The access that we have is so beautiful and beneficial; it is almost poetic, and I know many readers feel the same way. It is wonderful to know that, today, we have the choice to collectively agree to the user-friendly Donum principles outlined in this book. Together, we *can* create greater gifting enjoyment and satisfaction while lengthening the life of our planet Earth.

Points to Ponder

● There are almost endless amounts of items on the market, each with mind-numbing variations. This decision fatigue means there is a greater chance of selecting the wrong gift anytime you just begin Googling. So, pre-plan and don't go down the misgifting rabbit hole.

● Creating a sustainable gifting experience takes a little bit of effort on the front end, but your efforts will provide lasting results on the back end.

● Thoughtful shopping includes thinking outside the box for those who are hard to shop for, seem to have everything they need, who want for very little, who already have a lot of stuff, minimalists, and those who have evolved into a season of life where they are typically no longer in an accumulation phase of life. It is important to refine our gifting practices as those that we buy for develop and change how they live.

● Thoughtful shopping includes considering where products are made and what they are made from.

● Thoughtful shopping is a critical component to sustainable gifting as a collective society. It involves:

   ● consolidating purchasing into one trip or shipment vs. demanding we get everything shipped to us piece by piece.

- supporting companies who are endeavoring to do the right thing.

- endeavoring to shop locally and seasonally, supporting local farmers, ranchers, and dairy producers. With minimal effort, you can purchase local meat, eggs, milk, and produce.

- knowing who you are buying for. Grabbing an item off a shelf without any guarantee that they will like it, love it, or use it, is a waste, and it is the basis of the reverse logistics problem we are facing in the world today. Stop it. Ask them what they really want – it is a phenomenal question.

- Do not be concerned with surprising others as much as you are concerned with pleasing them and creating a pleasurable experience.

- Do not be concerned with underspending. Once you begin leveraging the Donum principles, whether via app or interviewing those in your tribe, your misgifting problems will be solved. Most people have wonderful items that they would love to have that fit into almost any budget.

- Unthoughtful shopping affects all of us in the form of higher prices and increased use of natural resources. Amazon now offers a Monday delivery service for all of the items you order within the week. If you choose this option, your shipments are combined into as few boxes as possible, and all arrive on the same day. The driver makes one trip to your destination, not four.

Home products are thoughtful and practical gifts that are cherished by the frugal soul. Find out what types of laundry, cleaning, and bath products they prefer and buy 3 - 6 months of one item or mix it up and give them a bottle of each.

Shop with a theme. For example, this year, you might want to give green gifts or coffees and teas. Find out what your tribe likes and set them up with favorites in your category.

Gas cards and grocery cards. These are perfect for college students, young couples just starting out on their own, as well as seniors. They will be 100% appreciated and put to good use. Why? Because you are not augmenting their budget, but they still get to use the funds as they desire. My bonus mom received a $200 gas card that lasted almost a year. She said it was the best gift ever!

Charities. Find out what causes your person who has everything loves. What are they passionate about? What do they want their mark on the planet to look like? Where do they currently contribute or volunteer?

CHAPTER SIX

Message From My Father

"It cannot be right to manufacture billions of objects that are used for a matter of minutes and then are with us for centuries."

– Roz Savage

"You shouldn't have to bother God with everything. There are some things you can do for yourself."

– Walter E. Lynch

"I am surprised the environment is not at the top of the agenda. What is more important than food and clean air? We need a big push."

– Don Cheadle

The *sixth step* in creating a sustainable gifting experience is accepting a new seat in our collective consciousness where things have simply changed. And we must also. (written by Tracey)

My late father, Walter Elijah Lynch, was born in 1923, so he would be just about 100 if he were still living at the time of this writing. Yet, in many ways, he is still living because I communicate with him all the time - both he and my late mother, actually. In many ways, as I tell those close to me, I know them better now than I did when they were living. For it seems that as I get older and become the ages that they were when I knew them, I can process their actions, beliefs, and systems through a more matured mind where all the things they used to tell me now make sense.

My father grew up poor, the oldest of twelve children. Like many lay people of his era, he was an inventor, a repurposer, and recycler by nature and by circumstance. He was curious, helpful, and busy. As the oldest, my father felt a responsibility to his family and was pretty creative and persistent in finding odd jobs and ways to earn money. When he was about eight years old, one of his gigs was collecting glass bottles strewn along the railroad tracks. Sometimes, there were more than others, and he was always super excited when he could collect a few potato sacks full of them. He was out with his brothers Joe Louis and Bill one day, and they hit paydirt. The two sacks they brought were already filled so heavy they had to drag them. My father, not wanting to leave bottles behind, left Joe Louis and Bill there and ran home to get another sack. Boy, was he excited! On his way out of their shotgun house, his father stepped into his path. My father was excited, sweating, and in a hurry. His father asked him where he was going with the sack, and before my father could answer, his father took a fireplace poker and struck him across the side of his head, and knocked him out cold. His father thought he was going to steal something and use the bag to carry whatever that something was in it.

There were a lot of reasons for my grandfather's rage, fueled by the era in which he found difficulty raising his family and getting ahead. But there was no excuse. From time to time, my father would say, "I really could have been a great inventor... but I think it got knocked out of me." I tell this story because my father *was* a great inventor. He invented a contraption that could keep him on a roof while repairing it. He also invented the thingy with the extendable arm that allows you to change light bulbs you can't reach. He made his prototype from a broomstick, a Styrofoam cup, and a screw. It sat proudly for him and, embarrassingly for me at the time, leaned up against the wall in the corner of our kitchen. He also invented the sticky Velcro that became Command Strips. The thing is, he was resourceful and inventive, but he had not been provided a menu of possibilities for his life. He would never have considered pursuing a patent because he did not know the value of his ideas. He did not know he was ahead of his time. He could not have possibly known that his ability to limit the damage he caused by his minimalist lifestyle and subsequent carbon footprint would someday trend and that people would be called upon to evolve into exactly who he was, could ever be a *thing*. A simple man with big ideas, struck down for being ingenious: that's who made me.

In contrast, no one ever hit me across the head with an iron poker. No one successfully knocked my dreams out of my head, and I know he would be extremely proud of coming up with a system to solve a huge problem like unsustainable gifting and reverse logistics. My father invented me. I got his ingenuity, creative mind, and ability to solve almost any problem, and that is how this book made it into your hands. My father wasn't afraid of anything or anyone – not paralyzingly so, anyway. It took a long time for that fearlessness to synthesize with my voice and my passion to leave this world better than we found it and to solve big problems with sustainable solutions. Voices on each of my shoulders squabbled, caring not for the health of the brain resting between them. It was in the wake of these drowned voices that the courage to make this book emerged.

My father used to have a saying. "You don't have to bother God with everything. There are some things you can do for yourself." The older I get, the more I understand. We don't have to pray to save the planet. We have to act. We must use our common sense. He was the original rinser of plastic bags. We never used paper towels. We never owned a dishwasher. He was the dishwasher. That man would run a shallow sink of boiling hot dishwater and leave it in the sink all evening and dare you to drain it. That "good" dishwater needed to last all evening.

He cooked enough food for two or three days at a time.

He grew our food, prepared, and froze it. We were accidental vegetarians. He saved containers and repurposed them and was always wondering in the 1970s and 1980s when somebody was going to come and get these newspapers, paper bags, and plastic containers and figure out what to do with them. He composted, buried waste, and burned trash. This may seem like a lot since everything we do now competes with social media and entertainment, but there is almost nothing more satisfying than making your home largely self-sustainable, enriching, and environmentally supportive. We don't need to be perfect. We don't have to do everything. But we all need to do something. And that learning is alive in me today.

The average American produces 5 pounds of trash per day, or 35 pounds each week. During the holidays, that rises to 6.25 pounds per person per day, or 43.75 pounds each week. With a population of 330 million people, that means 2,887,500,000 more pounds of garbage are generated per week during the holidays relative to the rest of the year.

Perhaps another significant factor behind sharing this story and the premise of this book is that many of us feel *insignificant* or small – so small that we can easily believe that our singular actions will never create change.

The single focused action of simply knowing what to buy before you buy it, so you are sure the recipient will be pleased with your choice – this is a worldwide game-changer!

Adding a few other Earth savers to your repertoire will add fuel to your actions and exponentially increase your impact. But buying the correct gift the first time is the key to correcting the problems and lessening the effects the inherent issues of reverse logistics cause.

"Americans throw away 25% more trash during the Thanksgiving to New Year's holiday period than any other time of year. The extra waste amounts to 25 million tons of garbage, or about 1 million extra tons per week! If every family reused just two feet of holiday ribbon, the 38,000 miles of ribbon saved could tie a bow around the entire planet. If every American family wrapped just three presents in reused materials, it would save enough paper to cover 45,000 football fields." (Stanford University)

So with that being said, here is just one easy example that will help you increase your impact. After all of your gifts have been opened, sort through the mountain of paper, ribbon, and bows. Then salvage what you can to reuse: gift bags, tissue, boxes, ribbon, and bows. Place everything in a bag or container, label it, and place it with your supplies to use the next holiday. In our family, it is very common to receive a gift in a gift bag that you actually purchased and gave to the person gifting to you. We keep bags in rotation.

The Opportunity to Evolve

We are afraid of job shortages, elimination of jobs, eliminating our craft, and the way we are trained to earn a living. This collective fear is costing us, but it doesn't have to. Doing right by our people and by our planet will shift our workforce in the right place. We are afraid of losing trucking jobs, delivery jobs, and manufacturing jobs. We build less sustainable roads because we are afraid of losing construction jobs. We besmirch artificial intelligence (AI) because we will lose jobs in healthcare, manufacturing, and transportation. We are afraid of clean energy because we will lose jobs in energy and oil. We are afraid of meat alternatives because we are afraid of losing the meat industry. Our fear is causing us to protect old ways of doing things that are costing us our entire planet, not just our livelihoods. Jobs will always be created by progress. In order to make progress, we will need to overcome our collective fears that keep industries doing less, less quality, less durability, less workmanship, less everything just so the item or structure can predictably wear out, which will cause us to have to replace or repair it, which will maintain job security.

Animals adapt to their environment. They don't have meetings, debates, or summits. They migrate and they adapt, or they die. Humans can learn something from the animal kingdom. If you are a truck driver, you can adapt to the new transportation needs required to increase safety and maintain distribution channels without increasing costs to the consumer. When shifts such as this present themselves, instead of fearing them, we can learn and level up. Learn the skills of the next business sector that will need our truck drivers. Can ranchers move into the solar industry? Can truck drivers and train conductors move into electric vehicle manufacturing? Can healthcare admins move into a new industry that streamlines all of our medical data, removing the need for paper, repeatedly completing paper forms, manually collecting insurance information, and making phone calls to previous healthcare providers to collect records. We don't need to be afraid. We need to be proactive. We need to be flexible.

Animals adapt to their environment. They don't have meetings, debates, or summits. They migrate and they adapt or die.

We have the opportunity to be proactive versus reactive. We have the opportunity to preserve what we have and possibly reverse some of the damage we've already done. But by nature, without rules and regulations, we typically do what we want. And without a collective recalibration and realignment to create a shift in our collective consciousness, we will continue to be reactive. I have faith that the great minds of this planet will help us succeed, fix our problems, collect gasses and CO_2, somehow protect our rainforests, make shifts to more sustainable goods and practices, help us still live full and meaningful lives while becoming embedded with sustainable messages that retrain us to act every day and accept responsibility as the new normal.

We have faith that no matter what, the geniuses of our generation will rise to the challenge and beyond. But, while we are on our way to accepting our responsibility as normal and learning to act on a consistent basis by taking the preservation of our planet personally, access to many things that we enjoy as normal can or will morph by necessity and our need to survive. While we become more skilled at taking our global situation more seriously, emergency strategies may become a normal part of our lives.

One day in the not-so-distant future, these might be our laws:

- Limits on mowing.

- No grass lawns allowed. Only turf.

- No watering lawns or foliage. In this case, rainwater would need to be collected for gardens.

- Water meter limits. We will be allotted "x" amount of water per person per household at a certain price. After we hit our limit, the price increases. After we hit our ceiling, we are warned of impending shut off. Or water might be sold to our households in packages based on your needs.

- Electricity limits and packages with a base price calculated by square footage and inhabitants.

- Mandated electricity cycling based on capacity in your area. This means if it is 100 degrees outside and the grid is being overloaded, the electric company could digitally adjust the thermostat in your home for as long as needed to sustain the city or county in order to preserve its infrastructure. This option is now optional. But it will likely become mandatory.

- Natural gas limits and packages with a base price calculated by square footage and inhabitants.

- New home restrictions where only so many homes can be connected to the grid in each area. Any homes over the limit would have to be solar-powered.

- Solar power mandates.

- Higher taxes on gas and diesel-fueled vehicles.

- Community-based tool-sharing libraries where all types of tools and equipment can be shared by the community.

- Higher taxes and interest rates on homes and builders not meeting environmental standards.

- Fines for outdated, inefficient appliances, furnaces, and A/C units.

- Fines for high-flow shower heads and toilets.

- Mandates on how many SUVs can be brought to market each year, therefore restricting how many of each type of vehicle are in service.

- Restrictions on recreational vehicles, including private planes, campers, RVs, and boats. Incentives to convert recreational vehicles to solar and electric.

- Highway toll rates based on vehicle type (electric, fuel, size).

- Gas prices based on VIN number to validate vehicle class i.e., hybrid, vehicle weight, etc. (swipe your vehicle ID at the pump, the price is verified, and that is what you pay).

- Limits on annual flights we can take.

- We might have an ID that tracks our carbon footprint, which could impose taxes or fines and further limit our ability to negatively impact our planet.

Kids will be like, "Wowwww. That's crazy. Grass just grew in your yard like that?"

In the future, conversations will be had about how we used to be able to use as much water as we wanted. Young people will be shocked to hear it.

"You mean you could just turn on your faucet and let it run, and nobody did anything about it?"

"Yep, that's how it was."

Older people will say, "Man oh man. I remember when we all had real grass in our yards."

Kids will be like, "Wowwww. That's crazy. Grass just grew in your yard like that?"

They'll be told, "Yep, all by itself. It was awesome. Now we have to go to the park to enjoy it."

To this day, my father has a lot to say about preservation and conservation. I can see what he was trying to teach me. I can now see where I got my wiring for the environment, invention, and innovation. As humans, we wonder, how did I become who I am? What ingredients went into making me? Why do I even care about the things I care about? I can see the gifts my father gave me even when I didn't seem to care or didn't even know I was caring. Conservation, gardening, composting, nature, and minimalism is alive and well in me. Help me change the world by shifting one idea — just *one* idea about gifting. I am so proud of him and how he crafted me so well to raise the standard for my generation and our planet.

CHAPTER SEVEN

The Final Say

Message From Mother Earth

"We should bring in an environmental attitude, and I think luxury should automatically be about sustainability and quality."

– Jane Fonda

It's clear that our behavior — individually and collectively — is not, as we once thought, impossible to change. We can take drastic steps to protect our planet like we have for our health. In fact, our health depends on the planet's health."

– Jane Fonda

The _seventh step_ to creating a sustainable gifting experience is to acknowledge what the planet is saying to us right now. We must listen, digest, and process her needs, then take action. By doing this, we remain connected to the purpose of sustainability and why it matters. This connection will reinforce our modern gifting behaviors.

We could not consider this work complete without documenting a final word from our planet, Mother Earth. She is dying. How healthy she will be along her journey is up to us. Through conversations, we discovered that we both used to be fearful of her demise, which was a source of stress for us. We always wanted to do all we could to contribute to her health and longevity. It used to anger us when others appeared oblivious to the issues at hand and seemed not to care, but we have made our peace with our planet and our human nature and tendencies. We've learned to practice the art of allowing others to have their own opinions. We've learned that disagreement is not bad. It is not evil. Disagreement is only a contrast between what we want and what we do not want.

That is why, even though we are passionate about sustainability, we know that we cannot impose our opinions upon others to shift global thinking models magically. We can only share and align, then better coordinate efforts with those who care enough about this particular topic to kill a bad habit. Knowing we collectively have the power to evolve and assist in healing the planet is exciting!

The reverse logistics problem is real, and we do not believe it will be solved by corporations. We believe it will be solved by us, the consumers. The costs required to fix an issue of this magnitude will outweigh the cost of products with the increased workforce needed to make it happen. We will not, as consumers, pay the inflated prices that will result from "them" solving this issue for us. Remember, reverse logistics engineering is the process of trying to reverse the distribution of goods and attempting to get them back to the seller, but it doesn't work. If it worked, they wouldn't be burning inventory. If it worked, they wouldn't be dumping six billion pounds of waste every Christmas. Businesses know it is less expensive in the short term to send the customer a replacement and trash the original product than it is to process the return back to inventory and then send another one.

Trying to solve this problem by creating a manageable and efficient way of absorbing and processing returns is an unanticipated side effect of our convenience of shopping online without considerable thought and restraint. Think of it this way. If someone is growing green beans, once the seeds begin to sprout and grow into a plant, it is going to produce green beans. We cannot demand that green bean plant to reverse engineer its growth back into the ground. We can demand it. We can command it. We can pray that it will reverse back into the earth, but it will, under no circumstances known to man, science, or nature, reverse its growth pattern and return into the ground. We have two choices: we can allow it to grow and enjoy its fruits or we can pluck the plant out and let it die.

Mother Earth knows which of these scenarios is feasible – for all of us. She knows what she can bear, and she knows when there is no turning back. She is demanding we make smart decisions that can change her course. Simple, common-sense mind shifts can help preserve her. It is a beautiful thing to witness the United States as well as many nations come together to celebrate holidays and religious rituals where we unite in similar thoughts, deeds, and generosity. The feeling during holidays can be palpable, inspiring, and infectious. However, as the population of our planet grows, some of our former practices do not translate well to growing populations and the taxing effect that so many billions of people have on the planet by doing the same things all at once all around the world.

This one point should ring a bell in the soul of every environmentalist. Mother Earth hopes it does. She is calling for practical solutions and sound decision-making that fit within the existing structure of our customs and enjoyment. We believe that she is merely calling for a pause prior to purchase. She knows, in her great and infinite wisdom, that her days are numbered as are ours. But she knows how much she can bear, so she is looking forward to partnering with all of us so we can create and promote the same health and longevity in her life that we all seek for ourselves and our loved ones. With the same measure of care and concern that we consider our own needs, she is kindly asking we consider hers.

Our human bodies are amazing. Each of us is made up of ten major systems: skeletal, respiratory, reproductive, nervous, endocrine, cardiovascular, lymphatic, digestive, integumentary, and urinary. If any one of these systems is jeopardized, we visit our doctor. We seek advice, healing, and deeply hope or pray to be fully restored. But when Mother Earth has a broken bone, a tummy ache, or a fever that will not respond to treatment. We, as a collective, just turn the channel. There are many environmentalists and activists seeking reform, trying to draw attention, trying to disrupt our behaviors that lead to the symptoms Mother Earth exhibits. Their work is needed, commendable, brilliant, and focused.

We believe that if we come together and continue to design a path or "treatment" plan back to wellness, regardless of what big corporations choose to do, then we as global citizens, can be a powerful, persistent, and persuasive force in achieving progressive healing and stabilization.

If you experience severe pain, you seek an urgent remedy. If you break a bone in your body, you seek out someone to examine it and set it so it can heal. The bone is immobilized so it can heal properly, but if that bone is shattered, that calls for more intensive treatment. Pins and rods may be needed to reconstruct the bone and hold it together. We will do whatever the surgeon says it takes to save our leg. Our planet has broken legs. She has a fever. It is a living, breathing organism that provides a home for us. It breathes like us. If we smoke, we increase our chances of cancer. When we tax the planet with toxic gasses, its lungs, too, become susceptible to illness. When we invade it... infection – fever.

We must use the Earth for our survival. That is unavoidable, just as we use our bodies to experience life, but while we utilize its resources, we must do our best to care for its health as we care for our own. Our bodies will wear out and die one day. Our planet will too. We've made peace with that. But we can do our best to care for it to increase its health and longevity so it can be enjoyed for as long as possible.

It's heart. It's bones. It's skin. It's gut. If what we want in the limitless quantities that we want is too much for the planet, then we should adjust. Wanting everything instantly all the time, wanting everything we see in every color. Wanting for the sake of wanting things we do not even desire except because someone else has them or we can't resist what's trending — displacing our desires onto others and misinterpreting what they may like based on our own tastes and desires that typically will not match others. It's not okay. It's not okay for our planet to be in the ER. We do not collectively shift our consciousness about our behaviors by just calling 1-800 FEMA and putting the next ER visit on our collective tab.

Gifting is beautiful. The gesture of exchange can be a loving, nourishing act that strengthens bonds and creates memories, evoking joy. We are now saying, let us further evoke joy in this ritual by inflicting as little harm to our planet as possible. Providing joyful experiences should not hurt us or this beautiful place we all call home.

Next Steps

Our next steps are easy ones to take and no less convenient than our existing gifting practices. We are not victims. We are not hopeless. It is not too late to recover our awareness, love, and childlike wonder surrounding our planet and all she offers. It is not too late to rewire our minds, so the gifting ritual becomes resituated in a more comfortable manner for our planet to endure. It is not too late to reinvigorate our planet by tweaking our actions without robbing ourselves of all the fun. Turn on the news, and you will see that a lot of focus is rightfully placed on, "what if we don't?" We now have the hope of seeing one ridiculously simple way to solve a massive problem by shifting our thoughts. Now we can disrupt the narrative and shift focus to "what if we do?"

What if we do one thing that alters everything? What if we are brave enough to believe in Santa's folklore and giving principles? What if we are so cool that we decide to be intelligent shoppers that drive misgifting, not our planet, into the ground? What if we can share this message with everyone we know, and the scale tips our planet toward longevity and away from demise? Take the step to correctly buy the first time. Refuse to buy bad gifts. Know your audience. Do not guess. Aim for 100% satisfaction when you give a gift, remembering the gift is for them to use and love. The gifting act is for the giver to enjoy. This is just the long-awaited coffee break our world needs, and just wait, we've got another crazy idea coming after this one that will blow. The. Planet's. Mind.

ACKNOWLEDGEMENTS

To our environmental heroes:

Thank you to the many activists, environmentalists, scientists, founders, leaders, entrepreneurs, inventors, innovators, influencers, educators, and lovers of the planet. Abundant gratitude to these heroes and the many more who cannot be listed here. Every single one of you has inspired us with the courage to do this work. We are here fanning your flames as you have fanned ours. Without your brilliant work, we, as world citizens, would not have made the progress we have and could not hope to continue.

Aaron Fairchild, CEO, Green Canopy

Adrian Grenier, Actor and Environmental Activist

Al Gore, Former US Vice President, and Climate Advocate

Amelia Baxter, Co-Founder and CEO, WholeTrees

Andrew Shakman, Co-Founder and CEO, Leanpath

Angelina Jolie, Actor, Humanitarian, and Conservationist

Anselm Doering, Founder, President & CEO, Ecologic Solutions

AY, Artist, Entrepreneur and Sustainability Activist

Brad Morton, Principal and CEO, Mortan Solar & Electric

Brad Pitt, Actor and Sustainability Activist

Brandi DeCarli, Founding Partner and CEO, Farm from a Box

Brandy Hall, Founder and CEO, Shades of Green Permaculture

BTS, Musical Artists and Formula E Ambassadors

Cate Blanchett, Actor & Ambassador for the Australian Conservation Fund Council

Chad Farrell, Founder and CEO, Encore Renewable Energy

Chaz Berman, Board Member and CEO, Grower's Secret

Collin O'Mara, President and CEO, National Wildlife Federation

Damien Mander, Founder, International Anti-Poaching Foundation (IAPF)

Danni Washington, TV Host and Science Communicator

Daniel Silverstein, Founder, Zero Waste Daniel

Daryl Hannah, Celebrity Activist and Founder of the

Sustainable Biodiesel Alliance

David Attenborough, English Broadcaster and Environmental Educator

David Bronner, CEO Dr. Bronner's

David Orr, Paul Sears Distinguished Professor of Environmental Studies and Politics

Derrick Emsley, Founder and CEO, tentree

Don Cheadle, Actor and UN Environment Programme Global Goodwill Ambassador

Duane Peterson, Co-President and Founder, SunCommon

Ellen DeGeneres and Portia de Rossi, Celebrity Animal and Environmental Activists

Elon Musk, Business Magnate and Investor, CEO of Tesla and SpaceX

Emma Rose Cohen, CEO, Final and Advocate Against Single Use Products

Fabien Cousteau, Aquanaut

Frederico Garcea, Co-Founder and CEO, Treedom

Gaylord Nelson, Politician and Creator of Earth Day

George Washington Carver, Agricultural Scientist

Gene Gebolys, Founder, President, and CEO, World Energy

Gisele Bundchen, Model and 2011 Greenest International Celebrity of the Year
Graham Ray, CEO, DeepRoot

Greta Thunberg, Climate Activist

Hans Cosmas Ngoteya, Conservationist

Hari Balasubramanian, Managing Partner, EcoAdvisors

Howard G. Buffett, CEO, Howard G. Buffett Foundation, Wildlife Conservationist

Howard Zahniser, Architect of the Wilderness Act

Ian Urbina, Reporter

Inger Andersen, Executive Director of the United Nations Environment Programme

Jaden Smith, Actor and creator of JUST Water

James Hansen, American adjunct professor directing the Program on Climate Science, Awareness and Solutions of the Earth Institute at Columbia University

Jane Fonda, Celebrity Activist

Jane Goodall, World's Foremost Expert on Chimpanzees

Jeff Corwin, Biologist and Conservationist

Jeff Orlowski, Filmmaker

Jeffrey W. Eckel, Chairman and CEO, Hannon Armstrong

Jeffrey Perlman, President, Founder and CEO, Bright Power

JoAnna Abrams, Founder and CEO, MindClick

Joey Bergstein, CEO, Seventh Generation

John-Paul Maxfield, Founder, Waste Farmers

John Muir, The Father of National Parks

Jordan Ramer, CEO, EV Connect

Julia Hill, Environmental Activist

Julia Jackson, Founder, Grounded

Julia Louis-Dreyfus, Actor and California Coastline Environmentalist

Kate Williams, CEO 1% For The Planet

Katherine Wilkinson, Author, Strategist, and Teacher

Kevin Chin, Chairman and CEO, VivoPower

Leah Thomas, Environmentalist and Founder of Eco-lifestyle Blog "@greengirlleah

Leilani Munter, Race Car Driver and Environmental Activist

Leonardo DiCaprio, Actor and Animal and Environmental Activist

Lennox Yearwood Jr., Minister and Community Activist, Influential Member of Political Hip Hop

Malaika Vaz, Conservationist and Filmmaker

Marci Zaroff, Founder and CEO, ECO fashion

Mark Hertsgaard, Co-Founder and Executive Director, Covering Climate Now

Mark Ruffalo, Actor and Advocate against the Keystone XL Pipeline

Matt Damon, Actor and Water Environmentalist

Matt Hill, Founder and Chief Environmental Evangelist, One Tree Planted

Meryl Streep, Celebrity Activist

Miyoko Schinner, Founder and CEO, Miyoko's

Nana Boateng Osei, Co-Founder and CEO, Bôhten

Nancy E. Pfund, Founder and Managing Partner, DBL Partners

Osprey Orielle Lake, Founder and Executive Director, WECAN

Pat Mitchell, Co-Founder, TEDWomen

Paul Stamets, Mycologist and Founder of Fungi Perfecti

Paul Watson, Conservationist and Environmental Activist

Pete Davis, Co-Founder and CEO, GreenPrint

Peter Krull, Founder, Director of Investments and CEO,

Earth Equity Advisors

Prince Harry, Duke of Sussex

Rachel Carson, Environmental Author

Robert Bullard, The Father of Environmental Justice

Robert Redford, Actor and Environmental Activist, Trustee with the Natural Resources Defense

Rosario Dawson, Actor and Conservationist

Rue Mapp, Founder, Outdoor Afro

Russell Diez-Canseco, President and CEO, Vital Farms

Ryan Hickman, Founder of Ryan's Recycling

Sam Teicher, Chief Reef Officer, Coral Vita

Sebastiao Salgado, Brazilian Social Documentary Photographer & Photojournalist

Seth Goldman, Founder of Eat the Change

Shadi Bakour, CEO, Pathwater

Shailene Woodley, Water Advocate

Sally Ranney, Founder and CEO, Global Choices

Sam Teicher, Chief Reef Officer, Coral Vita

Stella McCartney, Fashion Designer

Steven Novick, Founder and CEO, Farmstand

Sting, Music Artist and Co-Founder of the Rainforest Foundation

Sylvia Earle, President and Chairman, Mission Blue

Tom Szaky, Founder and CEO, TerraCycle

Tony Salas, CEO Shared-X

Trevor Hardy, CEO, BlueWave

Dr. Venkat Maroju, CEO, SourceTrace Systems

Wangari Maathai, Environmental Activist

Warren E. Buffett, Chairman and CEO, Berkshire Hathaway, Philanthropist

William Nordhaus, American Economist

Winona LaDuke, Land Rights Activist

Xiye Bastida, Climate Activist

Yvon Chouinard, Founder of Patagonia and Environmental Educator

INDEX

Jane Goodall Institute

Maddox Jolie-Pitt Foundation

Oceana

Oceanic Preservation Society

One Tree Planted

Rainforest Alliance

Practical Action

Sustainable Biodiesel Alliance

The Ellen Fund

The Rainforest Foundation

The Solutions Project

Treedom

Union of Concerned Scientists

Water.org

Women's Earth and Climate Action Network (WECAN)

World Wildlife Federation

It is important to conduct your own research prior to giving to any organization.

Companies Offering Sustainable Products: Sustainable Gift Ideas

The 4Ocean Beaded Bracelet - $20

https://www.4ocean.com/

By purchasing this bracelet, you will remove one pound of trash from the world's oceans, rivers, and coastlines. 100% 4ocean Plastic cord; Unisex, waterproof, adjustable; Handcrafted by local artisans on the island of Bali

Avocado Bed Frame and Mattress - Prices Vary

https://avocadogreenmattress.com

Avocado mattresses seemingly have the sustainable market cornered on green mattresses. Their bedding is made out of certified, non-toxic, and organic materials. The brand is also Climate Neutral certified; their factories are powered by renewable energy and have set a goal to try and achieve zero waste in their production.

Bombas - One Item Purchased = One Item Donated

https://www.bombas.com

We make socks, underwear, and t-shirts. You, and all of our other customers, help donate them—fulfilling a real need in the lives of those experiencing homelessness.

The Detox Market- Meow Meow Tweet Deodorant Stick-

$14

https://www.thedetoxmarket.com

Meow Meow Tweet's baking soda-free stick might be the only all-natural deodorant that actually works (and doesn't crumble!). With a subtle woody fragrance, the blend is made from potent plant oils and mineral powders — all packed in a convenient push-up tube that's completely biodegradable. This natural deodorant from Ritual is also an eco-friendly option that doesn't sacrifice functionality and comes in a reusable glass container.

Girlfriend Collective - Various Products - 30% discount

https://www.girlfriend.com

This beloved sustainable athleisure wear is known for its leggings and bra sets made out of recycled polyester, recycled spandex, and recycled post-consumer bottles. The colors are delicious, their styles trendy, sizes inclusive (ranging from XXS to 6XL), and their packaging is made out of 100% recycled materials and is recyclable. Our favorites include the Dylan tank bra and matching Lava float ultra high-rise legging. The brand has also just added loungewear and outerwear to their line.

Goodwill- Various Products and Prices

https://www.goodwill.org

For 120 years, Goodwill® has been the leading workforce provider of job training and placement services in North

America, empowering individuals with the skills and job support services they need to thrive.

In May 2021, in response to the economic turmoil caused by COVID-19, Goodwill launched a five-year strategic initiative called Rising TogetherTM. This growing collective of committed industry leaders, including global leaders, philanthropic leaders and Fortune 50 companies, are working to empower more than one million individuals to connect with sustainable careers by 2025.

Green Toys - Fire Truck - $30

https://www.greentoys.com/collections/vehicles

Can you believe that this fire truck (which is a **Good Housekeeping Sustainable Packaging Awards** winner, by the way!) is made entirely from recycled plastic milk containers? Neither will the lucky kids who get to play with it.

The Honest Company- Products for Baby, Home, Fashion, Cosmetics https://www.honest.com

Health and wellness are a universal foundation for a life well-lived and I believe it's our responsibility to leave the world better than when we found it. We care about all people and the planet.

Hydroviv - Water Filters - Price Varies

https://www.hydroviv.com

Tap water across the country is different, so why should all water filters be built the same? Water quality issues can be impacted by a variety of factors including; the age of your home and city's infrastructure, the natural geology of the region, and your water source's proximity to industrial sites, farms, and military bases. Dr. Roy built a team of experts dedicated to solving water quality issues. Our Water Nerds lend their expertise in science, policy, toxicology, and engineering to create personalized water filters for each of our customers.

Keep Your Cadence - The Capsule - $14

https://www.keepyourcadence.com

This is exactly the type of knick-knack that you wouldn't think to buy for yourself, but makes for a perfectly unique gift for someone you love — especially someone whose daily schedules are marked by their self-care rituals. Each buildable capsule magnetically snaps onto each other, growing into a gorgeous honeycomb-shaped storage piece that can hold everything from lotions and medicine to jewelry and serums. Basically, one capsule is equal to one travel-sized bottle's worth of plastic removed from beaches.

Lettuce Grow - The Farmstand - $348

https://www.lettucegrow.com

Know someone who treats their home garden like their child? The self-fertilizing and self-watering Farmstand, which comes with more than 200 varieties of pre-sprouted seedlings, is the perfect gift for anyone who finds joy in growing produce in their own backyard. From kale and other lettuce to herbs, strawberries, tomatoes, cucumbers, and eggplant, the innovative gardening tool promises daily fresh meals for the entire family. Not only do the stands work for both indoor and outdoor use, but it uses 95% less water than traditional gardening. Plus, one Farmstand is donated for every one sold.

MVMT - Mvmt Minimal Sport Watch - $188

https://www.mvmt.com

Mvmt's ocean plastic edition is a sustainable and innovative ode to the ocean sourced by the Swiss-based Tide Ocean organization. The case, strap, and buckle are all made out of reclaimed ocean pollution and even features a solar panel underneath the dial that converts light into energy to charge its battery.

Natura - EKOS TUKUMÃ BODY LOTION - $27
https://www.naturabrasil.com/collections/lotions-creams

For those who need a little pampering, this body lotion from Brazilian cosmetics company Natura is the perfect self-care gift. It's another winner of our Sustainable Innovation Awards for using bottles and refills that contain 100% post-consumer recycled materials.

Nordic By Nature - Reusable Sandwich/Snack Bags - $17.99
https://www.nordicbynaturebags.com/collections/4-pack-reusable-sandwich-snack-bags

We have created lunch and sandwich bags that keep your food fresh, delicious and appetizing. The best part is that we all start limiting the use of non-recyclable plastic bags with our food-safe, non-toxic, phthalate-free, lead-free, and BPA-free sandwich bags.

Once Upon A Child- Gently Used Kids Stuff

https://www.onceuponachild.com

Trying to live a more sustainable life is not as easy as we would like it to be. Trying to recycle more at home, figuring out what is compost and what is not after eating at your favorite quick-serve restaurant. Add some kids to the mix and it becomes even more difficult to think about making the world we live in a better place.

We at Once Upon A Child are trying to make that a little bit easier for you. We do that by providing a great selection of gently used kid's clothes, shoes, toys, furniture and baby gear. Just by buying and selling these items at our stores, you are taking sustainable actions while saving up to 70% off retail!

When you bring in your gently used kid's clothing, toys and furniture, you are helping make the earth a better place. Recycling clothing can save thousands of gallons of water and millions of barrels of oil. Selling your gently used items to our stores allows other kids to enjoy them again. That helps cut down the emissions of toxic chemicals and gasses that are generated when new textiles and other materials are created to make brand new toys and baby gear.

Our Daily Wines - Organic Cabernet Sauvignon - $10

https://www.ourdailywines.com

Our Daily Wines has been at the forefront of sustainable farming practices since its founding in 1989, using nutrient-rich and erosion-resistant soils to produce vibrant tasting grapes — using far less irrigation than traditional methods. You also don't have to worry about the use of harmful pesticides since their cover crops create biodiversity by attracting natural predators like ladybugs and honeybees instead.

Patagonia - Women's Downdrift Jacket - $329 https://www.patagonia.com/product/womens-downdrift-jacket/20625.html

A winner of Good Housekeeping's 2021 Sustainable Innovation Awards, Patagonia's NetPlus fabric coats are not only the perfect warm outerwear — they're also made from recycled discarded fishing nets collected from fishing communities in South America.

Play It Again Sports- New and Used Fitness Equipment https://www.playitagainsports.com

You may never outgrow your favorite sports — but you may outgrow your equipment. Your locally owned Play It Again Sports provides an easy way to sell your quality used sports and fitness gear and get paid on the spot, or trade up for what you need now. Not only will you save with affordable used gear, but we also supply the latest new equipment and accessories from the most popular brands.

Paravel- Aviation Carbon Neutral Luggage Set- $700
https://www.tourparavel.com

To make these suitcases carbon-neutral, we offset all of the emissions that come from sourcing, assembly, shipping, and their final delivery to you. We also offset the estimated carbon emissions of your first trip with the Aviator, so that its first journey is as gentle on the Earth as possible. These suitcases incorporate sustainable and recycled materials wherever possible: recycled polycarbonate shells, recycled zippers, linings made from recycled plastic bottles, recycled vegan leather trims, and telescopic handles made from recycled, aircraft-grade aluminum.

Etsy - Recycled Notebook - $25

https://www.etsy.com

This notebook not only has a pretty cover design that gives ode to the earth — it's also made from 100 percent recycled paper and printed with soy inks.

SmartGlassKp - Etsy - Sea Glass Necklace - $46

https://www.etsy.com

Made from recycled glass bottles, this gorgeous sea glass-styled necklace is the perfect sustainable gift for anyone who loves jewelry. Plus, you can choose from five beautiful colors!

Stasher - Stasher Starter Kit - $93

https://www.stasherbag.com

The sustainable choice can also be the convenient choice. Stasher promotes a no-waste lifestyle while also providing a seamless way to store food and snacks. Their patented Pinch-Loc seal ensures a completely leak-free design, made out of reusable platinum silicone in dozens of gorgeous pastel hues. According to Stasher, one pouch replaces 260 single-use plastic bags every year. Plus, they give back 1% of all sales to nonprofits working to protect the planet.

Stella McCartney - Fantasia Pinstripe Fringe Shirt - $995

https://www.stellamccartney.com

Our latest unisex capsule blends fashion and fantasy, escaping reality through conscious wardrobe staples featuring new Disney Fantasia prints, original graphics, and vibrant psychedelia – bringing together two of the world's most iconic creative forces around shared values and ageless visuals from the classic animated film. McCartney is a firm supporter of animal rights, environmentalism, and is particularly known for her use of vegetarian and animal-free alternatives in her work.

Sunski - Sunglasses - 25% Discount

https://www.sunski.com

Constructed out of recycled plastic from landfills, Sunski

sunglasses offer a variety of styles of specs, from polarized shades to blue light blockers. Our standouts include the Avilas and the tortoise Seaflips.

Supernatural - Supernatural Cleaning Starter Kit - $52.50

https://www.supernatural.com

This cleaning starter pack contains four formulas made entirely out of non-toxic and eco-friendly ingredients such as plants, minerals, and essential oils. Their 13 oz reusable glass bottles are filled with concentrates for every type of material and surface: wood floors, glass mirrors, bath tiles, and granite counters.

Uncommon Goods - Socks That Plant Trees - $15

https://www.uncommongoods.com

Not only are these socks made with organic cotton, they also go towards a great environmental cause: Buying a pair will give $1 (enough to plant ten trees!) to a non-profit called Trees for the Future, which focuses on reforestation and helping communities across sub-Saharan Africa.

Versed - 5 piece gift set - $35

https://www.versedskin.com

The popular clean skincare brand Versed does all the work for you, promising vegan and cruelty-free formulas, in addition to recyclable and PCR packaging to maintain net-neutral carbon emissions. This limited-edition five-piece set includes the brand's best-selling products for a comprehensive am-pm routine: Day Dissolve, Weekend Glow, Just Breathe, Press Restart and Dew Point.

ENDNOTES

"Climate Change and Health." who.int. October 30, 2021. https://doi.org/https://www.who.int/news-room/fact-sheets/detail/climate-change-and-health.

"As retailers struggle to handle holiday gift returns, some turn to tech for faster and more sustainable options." https://www.cbsnews.com/news/holiday-gift-returns-online-shopping-optoro-retailers/. December 27, 2021. https://doi.org/https://www.cbsnews.com/news/holiday-gift-returns-online-shopping-optoro-retailers/.

"$428 Billion in Merchandise Returned in 2020." https://www.nrf.com. January 11, 2021. https://doi.org/https://nrf.com/media-center/press-releases/428-billion-merchandise-returned-2020#:~:text=WASHINGTON%20%E2%80%94%20Consumers%20returned%20an%20estimated,U.S.%20retail%20sales%20in%202020.

Almendral, Aurora. "Retailers are pre-empting a deluge of Christmas returns with an unpublished policy." https://www.qz.com. December 23, 2021. https://doi.org/https://qz.com/2106474/retailers-are-quietly-offering-a-keep-it-christmas-return-policy.

Schoolov, Katie. "What really happens to Amazon returns." https://www.cnbc.com. January 28, 2022. https://doi.org/https://www.cnbc.com/2022/01/28/amazon-returns-what-really-happens-to-them.html.

Schoolov, Katie. "As retailers struggle to handle holiday gift returns, some turn to tech for faster and more sustainable options." https://www.cbsnews.com. December 27, 2021. https://doi.org/https://www.cbsnews.com/news/holiday-gift-returns-online-shopping-optoro-retailers/.

Kealty, Ceire. "Returning unwanted gifts? Consider the true environmental cost." https://www.ncronline.org. January 14, 2022. https://doi.org/https://www.ncronline.org/news/earthbeat/returning-unwanted-gifts-consider-true-environmental-cost.

Segran, Elizabeth. "Holiday gift returns are an environmental nightmare. Here are 5 ways to avoid them." https://www.fastcompany.com. November 26, 2021. https://doi.org/https://www.fastcompany.com/90699840/holiday-gift-returns-are-an-environmental-nightmare-here-are-5-ways-to-avoid-them.

Almendral, Aurora. "Retailers are pre-empting a deluge of Christmas returns with an unpublished policy." https://www.qz.com. December 23, 2021. https://doi.org/https://qz.com/2106474/retailers-are-quietly-offering-a-keep-it-christmas-return-policy.

Staff, Brightly. "How Wasteful Are the Holidays?" https://www.brightly.eco. December 20, 2021. https://doi.org/https://brightly.eco/blog/holiday-waste-generation-and-prevention.

Sweeney, Erica. "How Holiday Gift Waste Impacts the Environment." https://www.discovermagazine.com. December 26, 2021. https://doi.org/https://www.discovermagazine.com/planet-earth/how-holiday-gift-waste-impacts-the-environment.

"Reducing and Reusing Basics." https://www.epa.gov. March 25, 2022. https://doi.org/https://www.epa.gov/recycle/reducing-and-reusing-basics.

Broom, Douglas. "Christmas, by the numbers: 5 facts about holiday season spending." https://www.weforum.org. December 20, 2019. https://doi.org/https://www.weforum.org/agenda/2019/12/christmas-holiday-season-shopping-retail-gifts/.

"Extreme hunger has more than doubled in 10 of the world's worst climate hotspots over past six years." https://www.oxfam.org. September 16, 2022. https://doi.org/https://www.oxfam.org/en/press-releases/extreme-hunger-has-more-doubled-10-worlds-worst-climate-hotspots-over-past-six-years#:~:text=The%20brief%20%2D%20Hunger%20in%20a,over%20the%20last%20two%20decades.

BigRentz. "American Wasteland: Which States Produce the Most Trash?" https://www.bigrentz.com. July 21, 2020.

https://doi.org/https://www.bigrentz.com/blog/which-states-produce-most-trash

Weinshall-Margel, Keren, and John Shapard. "Overlooked factors in the analysis of parole decisions." https://www.pubmed.ncbi.nlm.nih.gov. October 18, 2011. https://doi.org/https://pubmed.ncbi.nlm.nih.gov/2198778 8/.

www.ingramcontent.com/pod-product-compliance
Lightning Source LLC
Chambersburg PA
CBHW071808090426
42737CB00012B/1992